Pillars of the ~~Community~~

Henrik Ibsen (1828–1906), Norwegian poet and playwright, one of the shapers of modern theatre, who tempered naturalism with an understanding of social responsibility and individual psychology. His earliest major plays, *Brand* (1866) and *Peer Gynt* (1867), were large-scale verse dramas, but with *Pillars of the Community* (1877) he began to explore contemporary issues, and there followeded *A Doll's House* (1879), *Ghosts* (1881) and *An Enemy of the People* (1882). A richer understanding of the complexity of human impulses marks such later works as *The Wild Duck* (1885), *Rosmersholm* (1886), *Hedda Gabler* (1890) and *The Master Builder* (1892), while the imminence of mortality overshadows his last great plays, *John Gabriel Borkman* (1896) and *When We Dead Awaken* (1899).

Samuel Adamson was Pearson Writer in Residence at the Bush Theatre, London, 1997–8, and has taught Theatre Studies at Duke University, North Carolina. His plays include *Clocks and Whistles* (Bush), *Grace Note* (Peter Hall Company/Old Vic, *The Playhousekeepers* (Private Drama) and *Drink, Dance, Laugh and Lie* (Bush/Channel 4). His radio plays include *Tomorrow Week* (Radio 3) and an adaptation of Schnitzler's *Professor Bernhardi* (Radio 3/ Dumbfounded Theatre/Arcola). Other adaptations include Chekhov's *Three Sisters* (Oxford Stage Company tour/ Whitehall Theatre), *The Cherry Orchard* (OSC UK tour/ Riverside Studios), Ibsen's *A Doll's House* (Southwark Playhouse) and Bernhard Studlar's *Vienna Dreaming* (NT Studio). He is adapting Pedro Almodóvar's Oscar-winning film *All About My Mother* for the stage.

also by Samuel Adamson

DRINK, DANCE, LAUGH AND LIE

HENRIK IBSEN

Pillars of the Community

in a new version by
Samuel Adamson

faber and faber

First published in 2005
by Faber and Faber Limited
3 Queen Square, London WCIN 3AU

Typeset by Country Setting, Kingsdown, Kent CT14 8ES
Printed in England by Mackays of Chatham plc, Chatham, Kent

A CIP record for this book
is available from the British Library

ISBN 0-571-23155-1

2 4 6 8 10 9 7 5 3 1

Thanks to Jack Bradley, Nicholas Hytner,
Charlotte Barslund and the NT Studio

Special thanks to to Marianne Elliott

Samuel Adamson
London, September 2005

Pillars of the Community in this version was first
performed in the Lyttelton auditorium of the National
Theatre, London, on 1 November 2005. The cast was
as follows:

Karsten Bernick Damian Lewis
Betty Geraldine Alexander
Olaf Jack Stanley, Hugh Wyld
Marta Bernick Brid Brennan
Johan Tønnesen Joseph Millson
Lona Hessel Lesley Manville
Hilmar Tønnesen Justin Salinger
Rørlund Michael Thomas
Rummel Simon Molloy
Vigeland Tom Marshall
Sandstad Cornelius Booth
Dina Dorf Michelle Dockery
Knap Michael Gould
Aune Paul Moriarty
Mrs Rummel Annabel Leventon
Hilda Kirsty Wood
Mrs Holt Una Stubbs
Netta Jennifer Scott-Malden
Mrs Lynge Pamela Merrick
Ensemble David Baron, Ita O'Brien, Nathan Rimell

Directed by Marianne Elliott
Designed by Rae Smith
Lighting design by Chris Davey
Sound design by Ian Dickinson
Music by Olly Fox

Characters

Karsten Bernick, *a shipbuilder*
Betty, *his wife*
Olaf, *their son, thirteen*
Marta Bernick, *Bernick's sister*
Johan Tønnesen, *Betty's younger brother*
Lona Hessel, *Betty's elder half-sister*
Hilmar Tønnesen, *Betty's cousin*
Rørlund, *a schoolmaster*
Rummel, *a wholesaler*
Vigeland, *a merchant*
Sandstad, *a merchant*
Dina Dorf, *a young girl living in Bernick's house*
Knap, *Bernick's clerk*
Aune, *foreman of Bernick's shipyard*
Mrs Rummel
Hilda, *her daughter*
Mrs Holt, *wife of the local postmaster*
Netta, *her daughter*
Mrs Lynge, *wife of the local doctor*
**Townspeople, Visitors, Foreign Sailors,
Steamboat Passengers, Servants,** *etc.*

*The action takes place in Karsten Bernick's house
in a small Norwegian seaport.*

PILLARS OF THE COMMUNITY

Act One

*A spacious garden room in Karsten Bernick's house.
Four doors. The first leads to Bernick's study; the second,
in the same wall, to other parts of the house; the third,
on the opposite wall, is the main entrance; the fourth, in
the background, in a wall composed almost entirely of
glass, opens to a veranda, over which hangs an awning.
Steps lead to the garden, which is bordered by a fence
with a small gate. Beyond is a street lined with small
wooden houses painted in bright colours. Summer. Every
now and then townspeople are seen walking along the
street, stopping to chat, going in and out of a corner
shop, etc. Inside, a gathering of ladies is seated at a table.
Betty is presiding over Mrs Holt and Netta, Mrs Rummel
and Hilda, Mrs Lynge, Marta Bernick and Dina Dorf.
They're all busy sewing. Rørlund is sitting at a small
table, on which are two flower pots and a glass of water;
he is reading aloud from a gilt-edged book: a word can
be heard occasionally. Olaf is running about the garden,
shooting a target with a toy bow and arrow. Aune enters
discreetly through the main door. Betty nods to him and
points to Bernick's study. Aune knocks, then knocks
again. Knap comes out with his hat in his hand and
papers under his arm.*

Knap Oh. It's you.

Aune Yes, Mr Bernick wants to see me.

Knap He can't, he's busy. He instructed me to tell you –

Aune If it's all the same, I'd sooner see –

3

Knap – instructed me to say: stop ranting at the men at these Saturday rallies of yours.

Aune Aren't my Saturdays my own?

Knap If you don't use them to turn workers into slouches, they certainly are. This carry-on about the new machines being 'dangerous' . . . what the hell's got into you?

Aune It's for the good of the community.

Knap Hmm, odd: Mr Bernick thinks you're sabotaging the community.

Aune Mr Bernick's understanding of 'community' is different from mine, Mr Knap. As Chairman of the Working Men's Association, I –

Knap What you *are* is foreman of Mr Bernick's shipyard. As Bernick and Company is the lifeblood of your community and mine and everyone else's, Bernick and Company is your priority. There you have it, Aune: Mr Bernick's message.

Aune In *your* words. I know what this is about. It's the *Indian Girl*. Damned American shipwreck. They want us to patch her up *their* way, but –

Knap You see, there you go again, another tirade. Stop the rabble-rousing. Aren't you needed at the yard? I'll be down there myself shortly. Ladies.

He bows and exits through the garden. Aune exits through the main door. Rørlund comes to the end of his book and closes it with a bang.

Rørlund Finis, ladies. The End.

Mrs Rummel There was a lesson or two in *that* book.

Mrs Holt Sound, moral, inspirational.

Betty Food for thought.

Rørlund A restorative to the poison in most newspapers and magazines. The hypocrisy of these trumped-up 'modern' countries. Their painted faces are a lie. They hide decay.

Mrs Holt Very true, Mr Rørlund.

Mrs Rummel Look no further than the crew of the American ship!

Rørlund We won't touch upon scum. Not that Americans from higher classes are any better. Imagine a suspicious place, where family counts for nothing, where sacred truths are shamelessly hacked to pieces. Itchy and restless, cynical and uncertain: this is the New World.

Dina (*not looking up*) But big things are achieved there, aren't they?

Rørlund Excuse me?

Mrs Holt Dina!

Mrs Rummel What do you mean?

Rørlund I don't think it'd be healthy if 'big things' became the rule here. We are as we are, thank God. Keep your community pure. If while we sleep tares are sowed in the wheat, yank them out, burn them. An impatient age may want to experiment with new things, but *we*, ladies, are not its laboratory.

Mrs Holt So *many* new things, though.

Mrs Rummel We missed the railway by a whisker.

Betty Thanks to Karsten.

Rørlund God, Mrs Bernick. Your husband was in the hands of a higher power when he blocked that scheme.

Betty That didn't stop the slurs in the newspapers.

Marta And actually, he blocked it on purely practical grounds.

Betty But, Mr Rørlund, we haven't even thanked you. It's more than kind of you to give up your time.

Rørlund What else could a schoolmaster want from his holidays?

Betty Thank you, all the same.

Rørlund We're all willing to make sacrifices for good causes, aren't we? The fallen women for whom we're working I see as stricken soldiers on the battlefield. You, compassionate sisters of mercy. Ready the bandages, dress their wounds. Heal. Cure.

Betty To be able to see everything in that beautiful light. A gift.

Rørlund I was born with it. Though it can be acquired. You just have to put your mind to something serious. Isn't that right, Miss Marta? You stand on *terra firma*, now that you've given up life for teaching?

Marta I don't know what to say. In the classroom, I often wish I were out there on the stormy sea.

Rørlund Temptation. You're speaking metaphorically, of course – by 'stormy sea', you mean violent world? Do you really prize it? Look to the street – see the sun beating down on those sweaty little men, tripping over each other's seamy affairs. We're better off here, aren't we, in the cool shade, our backs turned?

Marta I suppose you're right –

Rørlund Your brother's home is an example to us all.

Noise from Bernick's study.

Betty Who on earth has he got with him in there?

Hilmar Tønnesen appears at the main door, smoking a cigar. He stops short at the sight of so many women.

Hilmar Ah. (*Turns back.*)

Betty Hilmar, lovely, we're not busy.

Hilmar I'm smoking.

Betty Come in, I'm sure it's a very good cigar.

Hilmar It's a very bad cigar: I bought it locally. Morning, ladies. So, what's the upshot?

Betty Of what?

Hilmar Karsten's Extremely Important Meeting.

Betty I don't know anything about it.

Hilmar Think sleepers. Tracks. Steam.

Mrs Rummel You mean – the railway?

Betty No, no, *that's* all finished with.

Rørlund It was a resounding 'no' to the trains, Mr Tønnesen, as you know.

Hilmar I just bumped into Knap, it's all heating up again. Karsten's in there with a trio of town moneymakers.

Mrs Rummel I thought I heard my husband.

Hilmar Yes, Rummel; and Sandstad – you know, shopkeeper from the hill; and Vigeland, too, or should I say 'Pious Mike'.

Rørlund clears his throat.

Beg pardon, Rørlund. Everybody calls Vigeland that.

Betty Just when everything was so serene.

Hilmar Suits me. Nothing like a good fight, we could do with the fun.

Rørlund I don't think we need that sort of 'fun'.

Hilmar Depends on your constitution. A certain class of man needs a thumping good fight from time to time. But you won't find bloody noses in these dreary seaports; nobody here has what it really takes to – (*Glances at Rørlund's book.*) *Women: the Maidservants of Society.* What the hell is this sewage?

Betty Hilmar, be quiet. You haven't even read it.

Hilmar No, and I never will.

Betty What is the matter with you today?

Hilmar I'm sick. As I was yesterday.

Betty Didn't you sleep?

Hilmar Not a wink. I was out on my evening breather and needed to catch my breath, so I went to the club, where I devoured a book about an expedition to the North Pole. Nothing to get you going like men at loggerheads with Mother Nature –

Mrs Rummel *Their* adventures don't seem to have done *you* much good, Mr Tønnesen.

Hilmar Then I was chased by a monstrous walrus into the small hours.

Olaf (*rushes up the garden steps*) You were chased by a walrus, Uncle?

Hilmar In my dreams, you puny ant. You're not still messing about with that ludicrous bow? Get yourself a gun, for God's sake.

Olaf I wish I could –

Hilmar Anything without bullets is a waste of time. Damn thrilling to have your finger on a trigger.

Olaf I could kill bears, Uncle, but Pa won't let me.

Betty Hilmar, that's enough, do you hear?

Hilmar Fine generation. Talk and games. If you want to be a man, you're going to have to grow up and stand eye to eye with something dangerous. Don't point that bow at me, you bloody idiot, what if it goes off?!

Olaf There's no arrow in it, Uncle.

Hilmar How do you know that for a fact? Could be one. Get it out of here. Why don't you ride to America on one of Daddy's ships? You could join buffalo hunts and come to blows with Red Indians.

Betty Hilmar!

Olaf I could, Uncle! And I could meet Uncle Johan and Aunt Lona.

Hilmar Now you're just being silly.

Betty Olaf, go and play in the garden, quickly . . .

Olaf runs into the garden and disappears through the gate.

Rørlund Mr Tønnesen, you really shouldn't put ideas like that into the boy's head.

Hilmar No, no, wrap him in cotton wool like every other mother's son in this hovel.

Rørlund Tell me, why don't *you* go to America?

Hilmar In my condition? Not that you people remember I have a condition. Anyway, it's impossible, there is the community to think of; the flag of Idealism to hoist. *Someone* has to do it.

Raised voices from Bernick's study.

Racket.

Mrs Lynge Who was that?

Hilmar No idea. Headache. No consideration.

Mrs Rummel It's my husband, Mr Tønnesen. Remember he's very used to addressing large public gatherings.

Rørlund I think all four men are contributing to the rumpus.

Hilmar What do you expect, if the subject is filthy lucre?

Betty Industry is better than pleasure, I think?

Mrs Lynge Pleasure?

Mrs Rummel Count yourself lucky you didn't live here when *that* was the thing, Mrs Lynge.

Mrs Holt Times have changed. When I was a girl –

Mrs Rummel You needn't go back that far, Mrs Holt. Only fourteen, fifteen years ago, God forgive us, we had a dancing club, a musical club . . .

Marta I remember the drama club.

Mrs Rummel Mr Tønnesen's play!

Hilmar My what?

Rørlund Mr Tønnesen wrote a play?

Mrs Rummel Before your time, Mr Rørlund. And it only ran one night.

Mrs Lynge Is this the play you told me about, Mrs Rummel? You acted the part of the *ingénue* who fell head-over-heels with the strapping –

Mrs Rummel (*throws a glance at Rørlund*) Long forgotten, Mrs Lynge. Though the rowdy parties are *fresh* in the mind.

Mrs Holt Some houses threw two or three a week.

Mrs Lynge But there *were* plays, because someone told me about a troupe of actors who arrived in town and –

Mrs Rummel The troupe! Whatever you were told, double it!

Mrs Holt clears her throat.

I remember nothing about a troupe.

Marta There was sailing and rambling in the summers . . .

Mrs Lynge I'm sure I heard about a mad troupe of actors who practically held the place to ransom. Is it true?

Mrs Rummel I don't think so, Mrs Lynge, no.

Mrs Holt Pass me that linen, Dina?

Betty (*simultaneously*) Dina, it's time for coffee – would you check with Katrine?

Marta I'll come with you, Dina.

Dina and Marta leave by the second door.

Betty I think we'll take it on the veranda. Excuse me . . .

She goes to the veranda and lays the table. Rørlund stands in the doorway, chatting to her. Hilmar sits outside, smoking.

Mrs Rummel (*sotto voce*) Mrs Lynge, what were you thinking?

Mrs Holt Honestly, Mrs Rummel, you started it.

Mrs Rummel I resent that, Mrs Holt.

Mrs Lynge Did I put my foot in it?

Mrs Rummel To start jabbering about . . . with Dina sitting next to you.

Mrs Lynge Dina?

Mrs Holt And in this house of all places.

Mrs Lynge Don't tell me there's something wrong with her?

Mrs Holt Surely you know about Mr Tønnesen and –

Mrs Rummel Hilda, take your constitutional: the garden is so pretty.

Mrs Holt Likewise, Netta. When poor Dina comes back, be gentle. You know what I mean.

Hilda and Netta go into the garden.

Mrs Lynge (*surreptitiously points at Hilmar*) Mr Tønnesen –?

Mrs Rummel Not *that* Mr Tønnesen, he's Betty's cousin. We're talking about the *other* Mr Tønnesen, Betty's brother –

Mrs Holt Mr Tønnesen, the degenerate.

Mrs Rummel Johan. He ran away to America.

Mrs Holt Not voluntarily. If you see what I mean.

Mrs Lynge Something shocking?

Mrs Rummel Very. There was a – (*Clears her throat.*) *liaison* – between the degenerate Mr Tønnesen and Dina's *mother*. Isn't it funny how it floods back the second you start talking about it? Johan, the degenerate, worked in old Mrs Bernick's office. Mr Bernick had just come home from Paris –

Mrs Holt – he hadn't yet married Betty –

Mrs Lynge – and –

Mrs Rummel Well –

Mrs Lynge Get to the good bit.

Mrs Rummel – that winter the troupe of actors was here in town (yes, there *was* one) –

Mrs Holt – its star players: the Dorfs, Dina's father and mother. You should have seen the local men . . . drooling over La Dorf like dogs . . .

Mrs Rummel God knows why.

Mrs Lynge So –

Mrs Rummel – late one evening, Mr Dorf came to the hotel –

Mrs Holt – out of the blue –

Mrs Rummel – to discover La Dorf . . . I'm sorry, some things shouldn't be aired.

Mrs Holt Mr Dorf didn't discover anything, Mrs Rummel, because the door was locked.

Mrs Rummel Yes, precisely. From the inside. Picture the scene. The man in the room jumped clean out of the window.

Mrs Holt The *attic* window.

Mrs Lynge And that was –

Mrs Rummel Betty Bernick's brother, yes.

Mrs Lynge Who then went to America?

Mrs Holt What choice did he have?

Mrs Rummel It gets worse. It turned out before he fled, he'd slipped his greasy fingers into the Bernick Company cash box.

Mrs Holt That was never proved, Mrs Rummel, as you know. It might be a rumour.

Mrs Rummel For heaven's sake, the whole town knew about it. Old Mrs Bernick nearly went bankrupt because of it, and I had *that* from my husband's mouth. God forbid I'd spread a lie.

Mrs Holt In any case, La Dorf certainly didn't see a penny –

Mrs Lynge What happened to her?

Mrs Rummel After the actor husband abandoned her –

Mrs Holt – and his own daughter –

Mrs Rummel – she decided to reside *here*.

Mrs Holt The audacity.

Mrs Rummel She didn't dare show her face at the theatre, and ended up scrounging a living washing and sewing . . .

Mrs Holt She even founded a dancing school.

Mrs Rummel Disastrous. What sort of parent would let their child go near such a piece of work? Anyway, *la actrice* had never lifted a finger in her life and within a year it all got on top of her. Her lungs collapsed and she dropped dead.

Mrs Lynge How appalling.

Mrs Rummel Think of the Bernicks. The tarnish on the escutcheon, as my husband put it. So, Mrs Lynge, the moral of the story: hush-hush, in *this* house.

Mrs Holt And for love of God, don't mention the half-sister!

Mrs Lynge Mrs Bernick has a half-sister?

Mrs Rummel Had, not has. There's nothing between them any more.

Mrs Holt Lona Hessel. Unhinged. Lived only for herself.

Mrs Rummel She chopped all her hair off and clomped about in the thunder and lightning wearing men's boots.

Mrs Holt And when her degenerate half-brother –

Mrs Rummel – about whom the whole town was talking –

Mrs Holt – when he fled to America, what do you think she did? Followed him.

Mrs Rummel Well, there was the matter of her own humiliation.

Mrs Holt Sssshhh!

Mrs Lynge Her own humiliation?

Mrs Rummel Mrs Lynge, all things considered . . . I think it's in your interest to know. Mr Bernick had just got engaged to Betty, and the two of them came in arm-in-arm to announce the happy news . . . when Lona Hessel leapt from her armchair and punched Karsten Bernick –

Mrs Holt – well-bred Karsten Bernick –

Mrs Rummel – *thumped* Karsten in the face with such ferocity he saw stars.

Mrs Lynge I'm lost for words!

Mrs Holt Doesn't it stick in the craw?

Mrs Rummel Then she packed her things and bolted for America.

Mrs Lynge So Lona Hessel took a fancy to Mr Bernick?

Mrs Rummel She'd got it into her head that he'd been pining away for her in Paris.

Mrs Holt Ha! Karsten Bernick?

Mrs Rummel Man of the world –

Mrs Holt Perfect gentleman –

Mrs Rummel The darling of the ladies –

Mrs Holt Courteous, honest, virtuous –

Mrs Lynge Yes, yes, but what happened to Lona Hessel in America?

Mrs Rummel Over that, as my husband put it, a veil has been drawn, and one should hesitate before one lifts it.

They hesitate.

She sings for her supper in drinking dens –

Mrs Holt – gives public lectures on scandalous subjects –

Mrs Rummel – and has published a downright dirty book.

Mrs Lynge No!

Mrs Rummel Yes. Lona Hessel: the second fly in the Bernick honey. So, Mrs Lynge, now you know. You flew so close to the flame, I had to say something.

Mrs Lynge Thank you. Poor Dina Dorf! I feel so sorry for her.

Mrs Rummel Where Dina's concerned, I call it a stroke of luck. Imagine if the Dorfs had raised her? In the end it was Marta who took her in, though we've all done our bit to tame her.

Mrs Holt A difficult child, but look at the pedigree. She's not one of us, but we make allowances.

Mrs Rummel Ssshh. (*Loud.*) Dina? Oh, clever as a cat! And quite docile.

Marta, Dina and the maid enter with the coffee things and take them to the veranda.

Hello, Dina. We're just finishing up here.

Mrs Holt Delicious, Dina, I'm all for a cup of coffee at this hour . . .

Betty (*calls from the veranda*) This way, ladies . . .

The ladies seat themselves on the veranda and chat to Dina with a great show of kindness. After a moment, she comes into the room to look for her sewing.

Aren't you staying, Dina –?

Dina No, thank you, I don't feel like coffee.

She sits and sews. Betty and Rørlund exchange a few words, then Rørlund enters the room, finds an excuse to approach the table, and speaks to Dina softly.

Rørlund Dina. All by yourself?

Dina I've been talked about. It was written all over that Mrs Lynge's face.

Rørlund I thought she was very kind to you.

Dina Exactly. I can't stand it.

Rørlund Dina. That's a bit wilful.

Dina Yes. I can't help that, though. I was born that way.

Rørlund Hmm. You could change.

Dina shakes her head.

Why not?

Dina Because I'm one of the Fallen.

Rørlund Dina!

Dina Just like Mother.

Rørlund Who's been speaking to you about that?

Dina No one! No one ever does. Dina's much too fragile, she'll splinter to bits if . . . Oh, all this excruciating *goodness*, I could bang my head against the wall.

Rørlund Ssshh. It's understandable . . . sometimes you feel a little browbeaten, but –

Dina God, I wish I could leave. I'd get on perfectly well if only I weren't yoked to all these . . .

Rørlund Yes –?

Dina . . . genteel . . . moralistic . . .

Rørlund You don't mean that . . .

Dina You know what I mean, Mr Rørlund. Every morning Hilda and Netta are paraded in front of me, back and forth . . . Dina will never be meek like Hilda and Netta: Dina doesn't *want* to be. If only I could escape, I'd be worth something.

Rørlund You *are* worth something.

Dina It's poor currency in this place.

Rørlund You're not seriously thinking of leaving?

Dina If it weren't for you, Mr Rørlund, I'd pack my bags tomorrow.

Rørlund May I . . . may I ask why you like being with me?

Dina Because you teach me about beauty.

Rørlund Beauty?

Dina Actually, that's not it. You don't teach me anything . . . it's just that when you talk, you unlock something, and I see beautiful things.

Rørlund Such as?

Dina I don't know, really.

Rørlund They *are* religious truths, these 'beautiful things'?

Dina I don't know if they're religious truths, I just know they're . . . big. And not *here*.

Pause.

Rørlund I'm worried about you.

Dina I suppose that's better than nothing.

Rørlund You know how much you mean to me . . .

Dina If I were Hilda or Netta you wouldn't be so sheepish about it in public.

Rørlund Dina, you don't understand everything I have to . . . If there were some guarantee people wouldn't get the wrong end of the . . . I stand erect as one of the pillars of the town. The important thing is that you must, you will, be saved. Let's make a pact. When I'm able, when things have changed, I'll come to you and ask you to marry me, and you'll say yes and become my wife. Do you promise?

Dina Yes.

Rørlund Thank you, thank you, thank you; know that I love you, I do, I love you, I love –

A noise from Bernick's study. Rørlund starts.

Please, for my sake, the veranda.

Dina goes to the veranda as Rummel, Sandstad and Vigeland enter from Bernick's study, followed by Bernick, who is holding a bundle of papers.

Bernick Then it's all settled.

Vigeland In God's name, it is.

Rummel A Norseman's word is as solid as the Dovrefjeld rocks, Bernick.

Bernick No one's to give in. There'll be opposition, gentlemen.

Rummel United we stand.

Hilmar (*comes in from the veranda*) United? Against the railway?

Bernick No, Hilmar. *For* it.

Rummel Full steam ahead, Mr Tønnesen.

Hilmar Really?

Rørlund Full steam?

Betty (*at the veranda door*) Karsten, full steam? What do you mean by –

Bernick Betty . . . this won't interest you. (*to the men*) So, let's get the lists out, the sooner the better, and with our four names at the top.

Sandstad Agreed.

Bernick This is our duty. We're prominent men: we have to extend our reach.

Rummel The thing's as good as built.

Bernick Oh, I'm convinced of it. Work hard. Tell everyone you know. Men from all ranks, get them talking, then the town council will have to contribute its share.

Betty Karsten, you have to explain . . .

Bernick This isn't women's business, Betty.

Hilmar You've really decided to back the railway, after everything?

Bernick Of course.

Rørlund But, Mr Bernick, last year –

Bernick Was last year. *That* proposal was for a line along the coast.

Vigeland Ridiculous, Mr Rørlund: we have steamboats, don't we?

Sandstad It was much too expensive, anyway –

Rummel And it would have wiped out all kinds of businesses in town –

Bernick It wouldn't have benefited the community as a whole is the point. So I opposed it, and the decision was for an inland line.

Hilmar But that won't reach the towns around here.

Bernick It'll reach *our* town, Hilmar. We're going to build a branch line.

Hilmar Ah. A *new* scheme.

Rummel A damned good one, don't you think?

Vigeland The land is ready-made for a branch line: God clearly intended one.

Rørlund Are you serious, Mr Vigeland?

Bernick No, no: I have to own up to much the same thought. I'd *never* come home from up-country that way . . . I saw that valley and it hit me like a revelation: a branch line!

Betty But Karsten –

Bernick I commissioned a survey . . . here are the figures . . . there's nothing to stop us.

Betty – why have you been so secretive about it?

Bernick You wouldn't have understood, Betty; and anyway, no one knew till this morning. But this is the turning point: today the hard, honest graft begins. I'm going to see this through, I'd stake everything I have on it.

Rummel We're with you, Bernick.

Rørlund And you really expect benefits for us? From trains?

Dina We could go for railway trips on Sundays.

Marta Sssh. (*to Rørlund*) Weekdays.

Mrs Rummel Might butter be cheaper if we have a railway, Mr Bernick?

Bernick Mrs Rummel, it might be. You'll be richer, that's for certain. Progress brings prosperity. You won't know yourselves, the second that first train comes thundering over the ridge. And that land! Let me tell you, it's fertile; *finally* we'll be able to get to it! Think of an immense expanse of productive forest; think of rich mineral deposits waiting to be mined. Of the river with its waterfalls, one after the other . . . We improve the access, we harness that power, we build factories, right along the line.

Rørlund And what of improved access to the depraved modern world?

Bernick Ah, Mr Rørlund, the idea is new – so you're suspicious. Quite right. But you mustn't worry. Our busy town sits on firm moral soil; we can *all* take credit for pumping it clean. It's simply that your calling is different from mine. So, we men of business extend the town's wealth and influence – you'll still do your good work in our classrooms; our wives and daughters will still look after our homes and charities and husbands and sons . . . (*Looks around.*) Where's Olaf?

Betty Anywhere but here during the holidays . . .

Bernick Down at the harbour again, you mean? If he keeps chancing his arm, he'll break it.

Hilmar A little scuffle with the elements never hurt anyone.

Mrs Rummel Your love for your family is palpable, Mr Bernick.

Bernick Without family, Mrs Rummel, there is no community –

Knap enters through the main door with the mail and newspapers.

Knap The mail, Mr Bernick, including a telegram from New York.

Bernick (*takes it*) Ah . . .

Rummel Mail's here? Excuse me . . .

Vigeland Likewise . . .

Sandstad Goodbye, Bernick.

Bernick We meet again at five, gentlemen, don't forget.

Rummel, Vigeland and Sandstad exit via the main door, muttering 'Goodbye' and 'See you then' as they go.

Bernick (*at the telegram*) Christ Almighty –

Betty Karsten?

Bernick This is beyond the pale, even for Americans. (*Thrusts the telegram at Knap.*)

Knap 'Finish minimum repairs. Stop. Put *Indian Girl* to sail as soon as possible. Stop. Good season. In event of trouble, cargo will keep her afloat.' Optimistic.

Bernick *That* cargo! They know she'd sink like lead 'in event of trouble'.

Rørlund They can boast and swagger all they like: nothing will hide the fact that Things Are Rotten in America.

Bernick Profit. And not a second's thought for that crew. Can the *Indian Girl* go to sea in four or five days, Knap?

Knap If Mr Vigeland doesn't mind us stopping work on the *Palm Tree*.

Bernick Yes, well, he *will*. Open the mail, would you?

Knap Yes, sir.

Bernick Did you see Olaf down at the harbour?

Knap No, sir.

He exits to Bernick's study.

Bernick (*at telegram*) For pity's sake, eighteen men's lives . . .

Hilmar They're sea dogs, it goes with the territory. Nothing but a thin wooden plank between you and the abyss? – I like it.

Bernick I don't know of a ship-owner here who'd stoop to something so contemptible.

Olaf comes running up the street and in through the garden gate, holding a fishing line.

Oh, thank God . . .

Olaf Uncle Hilmar, I've been down to see the steamer! There was a circus on board, it's come ashore! Horses and wild animals and people and –

Mrs Rummel A circus! We're to see a circus?!

24

Rørlund I don't need to see a circus.

Mrs Rummel No, likewise, I don't need to see a circus.

Dina I'd love to see a circus.

Olaf Me too!

Hilmar Move on, weakling, nothing but swindles and swindlers. To see a cowboy tearing across the pampas on his snorting steed . . . now you're talking.

Olaf (*pulls at Marta's dress*) Aunt Marta, they're coming!

Mrs Holt Heavens, he's right.

Mrs Lynge How shocking.

Passengers from the steamer and a crowd of townspeople are seen coming up the street.

Mrs Rummel Definitely circus people. Look at that woman; can you believe her dress? And a knapsack on her back.

Mrs Holt Tied to her umbrella. Obviously the ringmaster's wife. See, the freebooter with the filthy beard.

Mrs Rummel Shield your eyes, Hilda.

Mrs Holt You too, Netta.

Olaf He's bowing to us, Mother!

Bernick He's what?

Betty Olaf, you're getting carried away . . .

Mrs Rummel Good Lord, now that fresh woman is doing the same . . .

Bernick She's what?

Marta gasps involuntarily.

Betty Marta?

25

Marta It's nothing, Betty. Absolutely nothing.

Olaf (*screams delightedly*) Here come the animals! And the American sailors from the *Indian Girl*!

Mrs Holt Even the coloured ones have come outdoors.

'Yankee Doodle' is heard, played on a clarinet and drum.

Hilmar (*blocks his ears*) Unearthly.

Rørlund Time to retreat, I think, ladies – none of this has anything to do with us. We have our work, don't we?

Betty I wonder if I should draw the curtains?

Rørlund You read my mind, Mrs Bernick. Allow me.

The ladies resume their places. Rørlund closes the veranda door and draws the curtains. The room is plunged into semi-darkness.

Olaf (*peeps*) Mrs Ringmaster is rinsing her face at the pump now!

Betty In the middle of the marketplace?

Mrs Rummel In the middle of the day?

Hilmar I tell you, if I'd been trekking through the wilderness and stumbled on a pump, I wouldn't stop to worry about what the natives – will someone please fling the clarinet player into the fjord!

Rørlund I think it's high time the police were involved.

Bernick No, no . . . foreigners. We mustn't be too hard on them. And God knows, we're used to rowdy sailors –

A strange woman walks in briskly via the main door.

Olaf Mrs Ringmaster.

The ladies gasp. Marta rises with a start.

Betty What do you mean by coming in here?

Woman Morning, Betty. Marta, good to see you. Brother-in-law.

Betty Lona!

Bernick Lona?

Mrs Holt God save us.

Mrs Rummel Just like a creature out of the sea . . .

Betty Lona? Lona?

Lona Yes, Betty, Lona: it's me. You can hug me if you like, I won't bite.

Hilmar Ugh.

Betty But, Lona . . . you've something to do with the rabble?

Lona What rabble?

Bernick You're . . . a performer?

Lona In what sense, Karsten?

Bernick With . . . the circus?

Lona Have you gone mad? Me, a fire-eater? I *have* made an ass of myself once or twice –

Mrs Rummel (*sotto voce*) Quite.

Betty Oh, thank God.

Bernick But the ringmaster . . . ?

Lona Yes, a real man, a sun-ripened man. Coincidence. We travelled with the respectable people. Second-class, but we're used to that.

Betty We?

Bernick We?

Lona The kid and I.

The ladies gasp, 'The kid!?' Rørlund flinches.

Hilmar Say again?

Betty Lona? A kid? What do you mean?

Lona John – as the Americans call him. *I* don't have a kid – at least I think I don't. Johan.

Betty Johan?

Mrs Rummel (*sotto voce to Mrs Lynge*) The degenerate brother.

Bernick He's here?

Lona Of course, I wouldn't travel without him, would I? Look at you all, so gloomy. Why are you sitting here in the dark, sewing white things? Who died?

Rørlund Madam, you find yourself at a gathering of the Society for the Morally Wounded.

Lona No? You mean to say that under those beautiful dresses these ladies have . . . *wounds*?

Mrs Rummel (*sotto voce*) I might have expected that from you, Lona Hessel.

Lona A joke, Mrs Rummel. It *is* Mrs Rummel, isn't it? And Mrs Holt? Time hasn't been so kind to we three since we saw each other last, hmm? Now listen everyone, enough of this: put the good work back in the box. The morally wounded aren't likely to die of their abrasions in a day, are they? I say we should have a party.

Rørlund Homecomings are not always causes for celebration.

Lona Where is it written, Mr Pastor?

28

Rørlund I'm not a pastor.

Lona You will be one day. Doesn't it all stink, like a shroud? I'm used to the wide blue skies of the prairies.

Bernick (*wipes his forehead*) Yes . . . it is a bit warm in here.

Lona Let's surface. (*Opens the curtains.*) The boy likes light. He's scrubbed up nicely, by the way. Clean as a whistle these days. (*Opens the door and windows.*) Well, he will be, if the hotel has soap. He got filthy as a pig on that steamer.

Hilmar Ugh.

Lona (*points to him*) Oh, look, it's *you*. He's still loafing about the place making unfortunate noises?

Hilmar I don't loaf. I'm ill, thus confined.

Rørlund Ladies –

Lona (*notices Olaf*) Betty? He's not yours? Hand me your paw, boy. You're not scared of your ugly old aunt?

Rørlund The time has come, I think; no more work today. Shall we meet again tomorrow at the same hour?

The ladies stand and begin to take their leave.

Lona Excellent idea. Count me in.

Rørlund Madam, what on earth do *you* propose to contribute to our society?

Lona Fresh air, reverend, great gusts of fresh air.

Act Two

Betty is sitting by herself, sewing. Bernick enters via the
main door, wearing his hat and gloves and carrying a stick.

Betty Home already, Karsten?

Bernick Yes . . . I've got a meeting.

Betty (*sighs*) I suppose we can expect Johan again . . .

Bernick It's not with Johan. (*Puts his hat down.*) No sign
of the ladies?

Betty Mrs Rummel and Hilda couldn't find the time today.

Bernick Did they have a particular excuse?

Betty Yes. They couldn't find the time.

Bernick And Mrs Holt? Is time also short for Mrs Holt?

Betty It is.

Bernick Where's Olaf?

Betty I let him go out with Dina for a while.

Bernick It didn't take that vixen very long to get friendly
with Johan, did it?

Betty Darling. Dina knows nothing about –

Bernick Then Johan should have tactfully ignored her.
Did you see the look on Vigeland's face?

Betty (*drops the sewing to her lap*) Karsten, what does
Johan want? Why has he come?

Bernick I suppose his 'ranch' isn't doing well.

Betty Yes, I'm afraid you're right . . .

Bernick They had to travel second-class, didn't they?

Betty But why has *she* come with him? After she assaulted you like a mad harpy –

Bernick Ancient history.

Betty It doesn't seem so ancient *now*.

Bernick Forget it, Betty.

Betty How can I? He's my brother, but it's you I'm thinking of; you shouldn't have to worry about all this. And then of course . . .

Pause.

Bernick What?

Betty What if they arrest Johan for stealing your mother's money?

Bernick Damn it, woman – there's no proof that money was stolen! None.

Betty But the whole town . . . you yourself said –

Bernick Nothing. And the town's talking through its collective hat.

Betty Yes . . . that's right, Karsten . . . you're a decent man.

Bernick I said it was history, Betty, stop persecuting me. (*Paces, throws away his stick.*) To turn up now, just when I need support. You're as bad as a newspaperman. It doesn't matter whether I welcome them with open arms or slam the door in their faces, every hack for miles is going to descend on me and start raking everything over . . . (*Throws his gloves on the table.*) And there's *no one* to talk to . . .

Betty Do you mean that, Karsten?

Bernick God, to be saddled with them – there *will* be a scandal, and it will have *her* fingerprints all over it. What sort of family –?

Betty I can't help that they're my relations. And I didn't ask them to come home.

Bernick 'I didn't write, I didn't drag them here by the scruffs of their necks' – I've heard it all.

Betty Why are you being so cruel?

Bernick That's right, cry. Grist to their mill, 'And then I saw the lady of the house, blubbering her eyes out . . .' Stop, Betty, what if someone comes in? Go outside.

There is a knock on the main door. Betty takes her sewing to the veranda. Aune enters.

Aune Morning, Mr Bernick.

Bernick Good morning. You know why you're here?

Aune Mr Knap said yesterday that –

Bernick You're not pushing on with things at the yard, Aune, and I don't like it. The *Palm Tree* should have been at sea days ago . . . It's not just me, I have partners; I've had it up to here with Vigeland's moaning.

Aune She can sail the day after tomorrow.

Bernick Good. And the American ship? Five weeks now . . .

Aune I thought you wanted us to get your own ship repaired before the *Indian Girl*?

Bernick You should have been fixing both . . .

Aune She's rotten underneath. The more we patch her up, the worse she gets.

Bernick Aune. Do you really think Knap hasn't told me what you've been up to? You don't know how to work my new machines. You don't *want* to know how.

Aune I'm nearly sixty, Mr Bernick. There are old ways . . .

Bernick There are – and they're of no use to anyone. Don't think I'm doing this to line my own pockets; luckily, I'm rich enough. This is for the town. I run a business; it has to serve its community. Progress, Aune. We'd be stuck in the Dark Ages if I didn't take the lead.

Aune I welcome progress.

Bernick For your own kind, you do. You're a troublemaker. All these tub-thumping speeches, stirring people up. Why? Here's a real step forward and you run scared.

Aune I am scared, sir. Scared for the men who'll lose dinners to those machines. You go on about duty to community; well, the community has *its* duties. I'm not going to thank men of science and business for forcing fancy machines on workers who haven't even been trained to use them.

Bernick You read too much, that's your problem. Stop chewing everything over, you might finally become a happy worker.

Aune Men are getting sacked. Men are starving. That's why I'm not happy.

Bernick A few copyists went hungry when printing was invented, didn't they?

Aune Would you have cheered for printing, Mr Bernick, if you'd been a copyist?

Bernick I didn't call you for a debate. Make the *Indian Girl* seaworthy by the day after tomorrow.

Aune But, Mr Bernick –

Bernick Both ships, you hear! These American louts have to be sent packing, they're no good for the place; have you read today's paper? Boozy brawling every night . . . and worse . . .

Aune They're a bad lot.

Bernick And who gets it in the neck? Read between the lines: they think we're fixing our own ship ahead of the *Indian Girl*, insinuating all sorts of rubbish. I lead by example, I've a reputation to protect . . . they won't throw dirt at my good name!

Aune It's good enough to stand this and plenty more, sir.

Bernick Maybe not, just now. This is a delicate time. Listen, Aune. Big things are afoot. I need the town's goodwill more than ever so that I can get what needs to be done, done. For the *town*. Some men out there want people to lose faith in me. I can't let that happen; I'll do whatever it takes to keep the newspapers on side; so you have to make that ship ready to sail by the day after tomorrow.

Aune You might as well order me to do it by this afternoon.

Bernick You're saying I'm asking the impossible?

Aune There aren't enough workmen. We're not trained.

Bernick Then I'll look elsewhere.

Aune If you mean sacking more of the older men, sir, you're *really* asking for trouble, from the newspapermen and everyone else.

Bernick You don't understand. If the *Indian Girl* isn't ready to sail the day after tomorrow, *you're* out of a job.

Aune Mr Bernick – (*Laughs.*) Are you joking?

Pause.

My father and grandfather spent their lives working for your family. I've been with the Bernick yard since I was a boy . . .

Bernick Who's forcing my hand?

Aune There's no way it can be done, sir!

Bernick Where there's a will. Yes or no? Answer, or consider yourself relieved of your duties.

Aune (*takes a step towards him*) I'm an old man. You think there's another job out there for me? Even if there was . . .

Bernick Don't think this is easy.

Aune You don't realise what you're doing. Have you ever seen a sacked workman trudge home with his tools? Listened as he tried to explain it to his wife?

Bernick I think I've always been a good employer?

Aune That's the problem: you'll come out smelling of roses, they'll think I asked for it. I couldn't bear that. I know I'm a nobody . . . but my home . . . that's *my* community, Mr Bernick. I'm the first man there and I hold it together because my wife and children believe in me . . .

Bernick What can I say? Big fish eat little fish. Individuals are sacrificed for the cause. Way of the world. You fool. We're not enemies. You just won't admit that machines are better than men.

Aune One old man down, hmm? Won't do you any harm. The newspapers will think you're doing what they want.

Bernick What of it? They back me, or they skewer me. Look. I prop up your house, and hundreds of others never get built. We could have a sea of new smoking chimneys out there, but only if I succeed in getting this scheme off the ground. So. I've given you your choice.

Aune Then there's nothing more to say.

Bernick Aune . . . I'm truly sorry this is the end.

Aune It's not, Mr Bernick. I'm an ordinary man, but that doesn't mean I haven't got things I have to hold on to. The *Indian Girl* will be ready to sail the day after tomorrow.

He bows and exits through the main door.

Bernick Stubborn ass. (*Smiles.*)

Hilmar strides through the garden gate, smoking a cigar.

Hilmar Morning, Betty! Morning, Karsten.

Betty Good morning, Hilmar . . .

Hilmar Oh, dear. Tears? You know, then?

Betty I'm fine, I'm all right . . .

Hilmar Then you *don't* know? The scandal beginneth. (*Enters the room.*)

Bernick Hmm?

Hilmar Our American relations are striding up and down the town with Dina Dorf.

Betty (*comes in after him*) Are they?

Hilmar Lona was so tactless as to actually yell my name as I passed. Luckily, I didn't hear her.

Bernick Others *did*, I suppose?

Hilmar You know what these people are like: twitching curtains, eyes popping out of their sockets. It's spreading like a prairie fire out West. I'm sorry, Betty, but I'm really quite worked up. If it doesn't stop, I'll have to take a very long holiday.

Betty You should have said something to Johan, Hilmar . . . told him that –

Hilmar In the middle of the street? No thank you. I still can't believe he had the sauce to show up. Well, the papers are going to cork his bottle. I'm afraid, Betty –

Bernick Papers?

Hilmar After I left you yesterday, I was feeling a bit under the weather, so I dropped in at the club. I entered to conspicuous silence, from which I inferred that the Americans had been *sur le tapis*, confirmed when that oaf of a journalist Hammer congratulated me at the top of his lungs on the return of my well-heeled cousin.

Bernick Well-heeled?

Hilmar His words. I shot him a spiteful look and said I knew nothing about Johan Tønnesen being 'well-heeled'. 'Really?' said the hack. 'Curious. People usually get on in America if they've a pot of money to start with, and your cousin went there with a colossal pot.'

Bernick You tell Hammer from me –

Betty Oh, Karsten!

Hilmar I didn't get a wink thinking about it, and now Johan's strutting about the town as blithe as a sunny afternoon. Why didn't he just bugger off for good? It really is irritating, how difficult some people are to eradicate.

Betty Hilmar, what are you saying?

Hilmar Oh, honestly, he turns up here in one piece after railway smash-ups and scuffles with Californian grizzlies and kidnappings by Choctaws – you'd think at least the *Indians* would have scalped him. Lord, they're coming.

Bernick With Olaf?

Hilmar Their dirty ploy to remind everyone they're from the best family in town.

Betty Look at everybody!

Hilmar Tramps, like flies. Honestly, I can't take much more of it. How's a man meant to uphold the Ideal in the middle of this –?

Bernick Betty, you *must* be friendly towards them: that's my express wish . . .

Betty Of course I will be, Karsten! I didn't think that's what *you'd* want.

Bernick You too, Hilmar: be nice. Hopefully, they won't stay long. But while they're here, the past is the past.

Betty Oh, Karsten!

Bernick We don't want to hurt their feelings.

Betty That's very kind . . .

Bernick All right, all right . . .

Betty I'm thanking you, Karsten.

Bernick Enough, Betty.

Betty And forgive me. I'm sure you had your reasons for –

Hilmar Ugh.

Johan Tønnesen and Dina enter through the garden, followed by Lona and Olaf.

Lona Morning, friends.

Johan Just been having a bit of a look around the old place, Karsten.

Bernick So I heard. There have been a few changes . . .

Lona Mr Bernick's good works on every corner. We've just been up at your park.

Bernick Nice, isn't it?

Lona Nice? Your name is emblazoned on the entrance gate. Magnificent. You seem to be responsible for everything . . .

Johan Handsome ships you've got. I bumped into an old school-friend of mine, captain of the *Palm Tree*.

Lona And the new schoolhouse . . . and they have you to thank for their water . . . and the gas . . . It's a real pleasure to see how much people value you. I hope I wasn't being too vain when I reminded one or two that Johan and I are branches on the family tree.

Hilmar (*sotto voce*) Broken ones.

Lona What was that?

Hilmar I didn't say anything.

Lona Perhaps you should have. Always good to say the first thing that comes into your head. Betty, the leading ladies of your Society for Moral Lacerations were at the market. We waved, but they were hellishly busy.

Betty Yes, no meeting today . . .

Lona Good! With your three frontiersmen and the pastor here, none of us got a chance for a proper chat.

Hilmar Mr Rørlund is a schoolmaster.

Lona Pastor to me. So . . . have I done a good job? Hasn't he matured? Who'd recognise him from that feral animal who scurried off?

Hilmar Hmm.

Johan Lona . . .

Lona Oh, so I'm proud? God knows it's my only achievement . . . the only reason I'm still allowed to walk the earth is you. When I think of us starting up over there with nothing but our paws –

Hilmar Hands.

Lona I say paws. Dirty paws. Bare paws.

Hilmar Bare?

Lona Yes.

Betty Would anyone like a stroll?

Bernick Good idea, I've got some time . . .

Hilmar *Bare* paws?

Lona That's what I said. He is a lunatic, isn't he?

Bernick Ignore it. You haven't seen the garden yet . . .

Betty Yes, Lona, we'll have a look . . . and Johan . . . it's not just the town that's changed. Come and see . . .

Bernick, Betty and Lona go down to the garden and are seen intermittently during the following. Olaf and Hilmar follow. Johan stays behind to remain with Dina.

Olaf Uncle Hilmar, Johan asked me if I wanted to go to America with him!

Hilmar You simpleton, you'll never let go of Mummy's apron-strings.

Olaf I will, when I grow big. You wait . . .

Hilmar Manhood will always be beyond your reach . . . no nerve, no pluck, no mettle . . .

They go into the garden. Dina has taken off her hat and is shaking the dust from her dress.

Johan Do you want to see the garden?

Dina No thank you. I've seen it.

Pause.

Johan A good walk?

Dina The best I've ever had.

Johan Don't you usually take walks?

Dina Yes, every day . . . but only with Olaf.

Johan So it's agreed? We'll take a walk like that every morning?

Dina Please, Mr Tønnesen, don't.

Johan What do you mean – did we make a deal or didn't we?

Pause.

Miss Dorf?

Dina It seemed like an excellent idea out there. But I've had some time to think and I've changed my mind.

Johan Oh? Why, exactly?

Dina You know nothing about me. That's all.

Pause.

Johan What is it?

Dina I don't want to say anything else.

Johan Please.

Dina If you must know, I'm not like other girls here. There's something about me. So no more morning walks.

Johan I don't understand –

Dina Or conversations, for that matter.

Johan *You* haven't done anything wrong, have you?

Dina Mr Tønnesen, I'm sure some other member of the community will tell you everything you need to know.

Johan Mmm . . .

Dina I do have a question, though. Is it really so easy to make a life for yourself in America?

Johan No, it isn't. You have to get your hands dirty. It's hard work to start with.

Dina I'm ready for that.

Johan You?

Dina I'm fit. And Aunt Marta's taught me all sorts of things.

Johan Well . . . damn it . . . come back with Lona and me.

Dina Please don't make me the butt of your jokes. You said exactly the same thing to Olaf. But tell me this. Are people very . . . are they very *moral* there?

Johan Moral?

Dina You know. Dutiful. Terribly well-behaved.

Johan They're not as evil as people make out. There's nothing to be frightened of, they're not ogres.

Dina You don't understand me at all. What I want to hear is that Americans are *not* very proper or moral.

Johan How do you want them to be?

Dina Simply . . . themselves. Natural.

42

Johan As it happens I think that's exactly what they are.

Dina Then it's my kind of place. And if I went there, I'd thrive.

Bernick (*at the foot of the garden steps*) I'll get it, Betty, wait a moment . . . (*Comes into the room to look for her shawl.*)

Betty Hellooo, Johan! We're going to the grotto!

Bernick He's staying where he is, I want to hear all about America. (*to Dina*) Here. (*Gives her the shawl.*) Go with them.

Betty Very well, Karsten . . . you know where we'll be . . .

She, Lona and Dina disappear through the garden. Bernick watches them for a moment, then closes the second door. He approaches Johan, clutches both his hands and shakes them warmly.

Bernick Thank you, Johan. Thank you. Thank you.

Johan That's enough . . .

Bernick Everything . . . this home, my position . . . I owe it all to you.

Johan Some good came out of the stink. Excellent.

Bernick (*clutches his hands again*) Not one in ten thousand would have done what you did for me.

Johan Karsten – we were wild, young; one of us had to take the rap.

Bernick But you were innocent.

Johan I was also free, no parents to shame. It was the ticket I needed to get out of that office. You had your mother . . . and Betty. She adored you. Imagine if she'd found out?

Bernick I know, but –

Johan Anyway, you *were* in Mrs Dorf's room that night to break it all off?

Bernick That crazed drunkard, pounding on the door . . .

Johan It was for Betty?

Bernick Yes . . . still, decent of you to do what you did.

Johan Karsten, I was proud to know you. The blade: home from Paris and London. I felt so provincial in front of you, yet *you* chose *me* as your friend. I know it was because I was Betty's brother . . . but there's such a thing as loyalty. Anyone would have done it. No harm. The town chattered, I got a passport to the world.

Bernick Johan. They haven't forgotten.

Johan It doesn't matter, I'm not staying.

Bernick Oh?

Johan My ranch won't run itself.

Bernick You're not leaving straight away?

Johan As soon as I can. I only came because Lona was homesick. Keep that to yourself. She's getting on a bit. (*Smiles*) She couldn't bring herself to leave me on my own . . . Johan the tearaway who at nineteen . . . well, who at nineteen *didn't* do what they say he did.

   Pause.

Yes. Sorry. I told her.

Bernick Johan –!

Johan It was wrong, but I had to. You've never liked her . . . but she's been like a mother to me. She worked like a slave when we arrived. When I was sick, she sang in bars . . . she lectured, was jeered at, she even wrote a book. She's big enough to scream with laughter about everything . . . and . . . the woman wanted to come home. So I had to tell her I wasn't half as evil as she thought.

Bernick How did she take it?

Johan She sensibly pointed out that since I was innocent I might as well come with her. Don't worry, she's not going to say anything. And neither will I. I never *have* . . . well, except to her.

He holds out his hand, and they shake.

Bernick I trust you.

Johan One skeleton in the closet – not too bad, is it? And it's all done with. I'm here to enjoy myself for a week or two. That walk with Dina . . .! D'you remember her in the theatre, running between her parents' feet, dressed as an angel?

Bernick (*nods*) The swine got himself killed in a tavern. She died not long after. You got my letters?

Johan Yes.

Pause.

You . . . you helped Mrs Dorf . . . while she was still alive? On the quiet?

Bernick She was a proud woman. She never said anything . . . wouldn't accept a penny.

Johan Well, you did the right thing by taking her daughter in.

Bernick I suppose. Actually, it was Marta.

Johan Marta? What's happened to her? She's so elusive. I've hardly seen her.

Bernick She must be tending the sick, which is what she does when she's not teaching.

Johan And she raised Dina?

45

Bernick She's prone to that sort of thing. It's stupid, really, this teaching lark of hers; I don't like it, it looks like her own brother isn't willing to provide for her.

Johan But Marta has her own money?

Bernick No. After you left, I made Mother take me into the firm – she'd made a real hash of it – and once we'd written off this and paid off that, her share came to almost nothing. By the time she died, there *was* nothing. Marta was left penniless.

Johan That's awful . . .

Bernick You think I let her go without? I say I'm a damned good brother. She's got a roof over her head, food from our table; her teacher's salary keeps her in dresses and things. What more could a spinster want?

Johan Hmm. We think differently in America.

Bernick I suppose you do, revolutionaries, taking up arms against everything. Ours is a small society, that sort of polluted thinking hasn't reached us, thank God. Women have their proper place, and they're happy in it. It's Marta's fault; if she'd wanted her own home she could have had it. She's had offers. Some surprisingly good ones, given how poor and old she is. Small fry, is Marta.

Johan Small fry?

Bernick Oh, I don't hold it against her. I wouldn't change her for the world. Always good to have a steady hand about the place. Someone you can rely on in a crisis.

Johan What does Marta think about that?

Bernick Marta? What d'you mean? Oh. There's plenty to keep the woman busy . . . me, Betty, Olaf . . . me. People shouldn't put themselves before others, women especially. Community first, however big or small, that's my creed –

Knap enters with a bundle of papers and Bernick points to him.

You see: am I worrying about my private affairs today? No. (*eagerly, to Knap.*) Well?

Knap (*sotto voce*) Sale contracts.

Bernick Good. Excellent. Excuse me, Johan. (*Sotto voce, clasps his hand.*) Thank you. Thank you. If there's ever anything . . . well, you understand.

He and Knap exit to the study.

Johan (*looks after them for a moment*) Hmm.

He makes to go to the garden. Marta enters through the main door, carrying a small basket.

Marta Good morning, Johan. Excuse me . . .

Johan Marta!

Marta Don't worry, the others are coming. We don't need a train station here, we already have one: this house. (*Makes to leave through the second door.*)

Johan Why are you always in such a rush?

Marta Am I?

Johan You did everything you could to avoid me yesterday. We're old friends, aren't we? They couldn't keep us apart once.

Marta Years ago, Johan.

Johan Fifteen, not so many. Have I changed that much?

Marta Yes.

Pause.

I beg your pardon.

Johan You don't seem very pleased to see me . . .

Marta Well, Johan, I've been waiting for such a long time.

Johan Waiting?

Marta Waiting and waiting . . . for you to come . . . come back and . . . make amends for your wrong.

Pause.

I don't think it's that easy to forget that a woman died in penury and disgrace because of you? And what about her daughter? Did you never stop to think about what sort of childhood she'd have?

Johan But, Marta . . . your brother must have . . . Karsten's never said a word in my defence?

Marta Karsten has standards, Johan.

Johan Oh, I know all about my old friend's standards. We've just been having a little chat about them. He's changed, hasn't he?

Marta Karsten is the same tremendous man he's always been.

Johan Yes, yes. I understand now, Marta. Now I see how you see me. The return of the prodigal.

Marta How I see you? This is how I see you, Johan. (*Points towards the garden.*) Look at the girl with Olaf on the lawn. That's Dina. Do you remember the rambling letter you wrote to me after you left? You begged me to believe in you. And I *did*. All those horrifying things that came out about you –

Johan What things –?

Marta For God's sake, not now . . . I put my hands to my ears. 'He's young, lost, stupid, of course he has to

48

leave and start afresh.' You see, Johan, I've been standing in for you here at home. Your duties – which you forgot or which were beyond you – became *my* duties. That girl was left for dead. But I became her foster mother and looked after her as well as I could –

Johan At the expense of your life.

Marta No. *No*. But you're late, Johan.

Pause.

There. One less thing to prick your conscience.

Johan Marta . . . if you knew . . .

Pause.

You're a good friend. Thank you.

Marta (*smiles sadly*) We've made a clean breast of it. Here they come. Goodbye. I don't want them to –

She exits via the second door. Lona comes in from the garden, followed by Betty.

Betty But, Lona, you can't be serious –

Lona Leave me alone, Betty. If I want to speak to him, I will.

Betty But it would be more than I could take. Johan, it's about to pour, come with me to the hall –

Lona Ignore her, John, it's beautiful outdoors and stuffy as a vestry in. The thing to do is go out and have a chat with Dina.

Johan I was just thinking that *might* be the thing.

Betty In the hall is a *wonderful* new –

Lona You've noticed her?

Johan Yes, I have.

49

Lona Good work, keep it up. Quite a catch, hmm?

Betty Lona, stop it!

Lona Go on, then.

Johan I don't need pushing, Lona.

He exits to the garden.

Betty Lona, think –

Lona She's in good shape, she's kind, she's honest, exactly the right sort of wife for John, perfect for America. The decrepit half-sister has had her day, Betty.

Betty Dina? Dina Dorf? Think, think –

Lona What I think is that she'll make the boy happy. And he *does* need pushing: no eye for the girls.

Betty I think there's copious evidence that Johan's 'eye for the girls' is the size of a ship.

Lona Oh, to hell with your daft fish-stories. Where's Karsten? I want to speak to him.

Betty Please, Lona, you mustn't.

Lona If he takes a shine to her – as they say in America – and she to him, it's a match. Karsten's a shrewd man, he'll have to find a way to make it happen.

Betty This kind of American behaviour will not be tolerated here!

Lona Oh, Betty, shut up.

Betty Karsten is an upstanding man –

Lona Karsten's been known to stoop.

Betty How dare you!

Lona I dare it, I dare to say that Karsten Bernick is no more upstanding than anyone else.

Betty After all these years, you still hate him. If you're not over it, why are you here? It's beyond me how you can look him in the face after what you did to him.

Lona It was disgraceful of me, Betty. I forgot myself that day.

Betty And he's forgiven you. *You're* the one who held a candle for *him* – Karsten is blameless. You hate me, don't you? You always have. You were always jealous. My life was blessed and you loathed me for it. You've come back to drag me through the mud, to show the whole town exactly what Karsten got himself into when he married a Tønnesen. It's me you're destroying, Lona; I hope it makes you happy!

She exits through the second door in tears. Lona watches her go. Bernick enters from his study, stopping at the door to speak to Knap.

Bernick . . . and that food for the poor fund, make it three hundred crowns. (*Senses Lona.*) Four hundred. (*Turns.*) Lona. (*Approaches her.*) No sign of Betty?

Lona Just left. Shall I call her back?

Bernick (*shakes his head*) We can talk. I've been longing to talk.

Pause.

Forgive me.

Lona Let's not get sentimental. It doesn't suit us.

Bernick I know you know about Dina's mother and me. And what it must look like. I swear, I lost my head back then . . . it was over before it started. And I swear I was in love with you once.

Lona Why do you think I've come home, Karsten?

Bernick Please don't do anything till I've explained . . .

Lona You're terrified.

Bernick Please . . .

Lona You say you were in love with me. You said it over and over in those old letters . . . maybe it was true, in a way: while you were roaming the big free world, you had the courage to dream big free dreams. Then I was your very own independent girl; out of all the grey folks back home, the only one with any colour. When I was your Paris secret, no one could sneer at your bad taste.

Bernick Lona, that's not –

Lona Then you came back and saw the grey homey folk heckling Mad Lona Hessel . . .

Bernick You were a bit . . . reckless, back then.

Lona Yes, because I wanted to put the wind up the backsides of the prudes around here. Enter the seductive young actress . . .

Bernick There was nothing in it . . . she hypnotised me for one moment, it was insane . . . and most of the talk was talk.

Lona Maybe. Then Betty came home, ribbons in her hair. Pretty Betty, loved by all. Betty, who'd inherit every crown of *her* aunt's money, while I got nothing.

Bernick All right, Lona, we won't beat about the bush: I didn't love Betty then; I didn't leave you because I'd fallen for someone else, I left for her money. I needed it. I I needed it.

Lona You have the nerve –

Bernick Listen –

Lona You wrote a letter! 'I'm madly in love with her . . . Lona, if you have a heart, please, please, *please* don't tell your sister about us . . .'

Bernick I had to –

Lona By God, I'm glad I thumped you in the head.

Bernick You don't understand. When I was in Paris, the house of Bernick was close to bankruptcy. My hopeless mother had succeeded in driving the work of three generations into the ground. That's why they rushed me back. No one could know. I was the son. I had to find a way to save it.

Lona So you did – at the cost of a woman.

Bernick You know Betty loved me.

Lona I wasn't talking about Betty.

Bernick You wouldn't have been happy with me, Lona.

Lona I see! You left me to make me happy!

Bernick You think I'm selfish. You're wrong. If the business had been mine and no one else's, of course I'd have let it fall and started over. But if a man inherits something, he has responsibilities: in the case of Bernick and Company, the prosperity of hundreds – thousands – of men was in my hands. For one second, won't you think about what would have happened to this town – our *home* – if my family's business had gone under?

Lona So you've been feeding off a lie for fifteen years for the sake of the Old Home Town?

Bernick Lie?

Lona Does Betty know about your merry bachelorhood?

Bernick Don't be gratuitous: you think I'd hurt her to no profit by telling her?

Lona 'Profit'? Well, I defer to the man of business: you know all about profit.

Pause.

Are you happy, Karsten?

Bernick At home?

Lona nods.

Yes. You haven't sacrificed so much for nothing. I can honestly say with the passing years I've grown happier and happier. Betty's a good woman. She's my friend. She's not so giddy about love now. She's humble, my influence. We set a good example.

Lona The citizens being ignorant of the lie, I suppose you do.

Bernick The –

Lona The lie, the lie, the fifteen-year-old-lie, Karsten.

Bernick That's a bit strong –

Lona It's not strong enough; a triple-lie, to me, to Betty and to Johan.

Bernick Betty's never asked –

Lona Betty doesn't know anything!

Bernick You're not going to tell her, are you?

Lona Don't panic, I can cope with the jeering mob.

Bernick Johan gave me his word.

Lona But what about *you*, Karsten? Don't you want to be free of it?

Bernick You really think I'd *choose* to forfeit my happiness? Quit my public position?

Lona You've no right to it!

Bernick I have every right. By the sweat of my brow, I've earned it piece by piece.

Lona Yes, you've worked. And all sorts of people have benefited. You're king crab, Karsten. You're rich and powerful; every citizen bows to you, they think you're flawless; your home is an example to them all. But see, everybody: it's a hoax! And if you don't do something to save yourself, it'll be one at your expense. One anxious moment, one stray word, and you will lose everything.

Bernick Why are you here, Lona?

Lona I want to help you.

Bernick Revenge is what you want. I knew it. You think this is going to work? Johan will sail back to America and these people will be none the wiser . . . and if anyone *else* accuses me, I'll deny everything. I'll fight. You won't get away with this. Try to bring me down and I'll fight.

Rummel and Vigeland enter via the main entrance.

Rummel Morning, my friend. Ready?

Bernick Hmm?

Rummel Meeting at the Chamber of Commerce about the railway?

Bernick Not now . . .

Vigeland Wouldn't do to miss it, Bernick.

Rummel The whispers have started. Hammer and that coast-line crowd. They're muttering that private interests could be behind the new scheme.

Bernick You can tell them that –

Vigeland Nothing *we* say will convince them.

Rummel They need to hear it from you, Bernick. No one would suspect you of anything underhand.

Lona No, no.

Bernick I can't . . . I'm not well . . . just . . . give me a second . . .

Rørlund enters through the main door.

Rørlund Mr Bernick. It is with some distress that I inform you that you are, this second, face-to-face with an exceedingly agitated man.

Bernick Not now, Mr Rørlund . . .

Rørlund Is it with your consent that the young girl who has found asylum under your roof walks up and down the streets in the company of the *very* man she should not –

Lona Should not what, padre?

Rørlund – the *one* man that she of all people should be kept –

Lona Spit it out, there's a good boy.

Rørlund – kept a million miles from.

Lona laughs. Hilmar enters from the garden and heads for the second door.

Hilmar Betty!

Rørlund Mr Bernick, do you consent to it?

Bernick (*looks for his hat and gloves*) I haven't got a clue what you're talking about. I've got a meeting.

Hilmar Betty?!

Betty appears at the second door.

Betty What is it now, Hilmar?

Hilmar If you don't want a certain philandering young man to philander with Dina Dorf, then look to your garden. Personally, I can't take another word.

Lona Oh, please turn the page on the tale, Hilmar: what's the philandering young man been saying?

Hilmar He wants her to go to America with him. Ugh.

Rørlund What?

Betty Dina –?

Lona Excellent.

Bernick Whatever you *think* you heard, Hilmar . . . I have to go –

Hilmar If you don't believe me, ask him yourself. Leave me out of it, please.

Johan and Dina are approaching from the garden.

Bernick (*to Rummel and Vigeland*) Excuse me, gentlemen, I'll follow you . . . one moment.

Johan and Dina come inside.

Johan Good news, Lona. She's coming with us.

Betty Johan, you're a thoughtless –

Rørlund This is simply not true. It is unbelievable. It is despicable. By what black arts of seduction have you –?

Johan Who do you think you are?

Rørlund What has he done to you?

Dina Nothing.

Rørlund You made this decision freely?

Dina I have to get out of here.

Rørlund This man – *this* man –

57

Dina Name another in town with the strength of character to take me?

Rørlund Strength of character? I think the time has come for you to see the true kidney of this man's *character*.

Johan Shut up –

Bernick Please, Mr Rørlund –

Rørlund No. This is my civic duty. I have a responsibility towards this girl. She must hear it. Dina. This is the man who caused your mother all her heartbreak and shame.

Bernick Mr Rørlund . . .

Pause.

Dina Johan?

Pause.

Johan Karsten, answer her.

Pause.

Karsten, say something.

Pause.

Dina So it's true?

Rørlund Of course it is. See it in his face.

Rummel (*taps watch*) Bernick . . .

Rørlund And there's more. Before you take his hand to go to America, let me tell you exactly where it's been. Ahead of his last voyage, he slipped that hand into old Mrs Bernick's cash box.

Lona Liar!

Betty Oh, God . . .

Rørlund Mr Bernick himself can confirm it.

Pause.

The truth is out. The whole town knows it. Mr Bernick corroborated it. Dina Dorf: meet the real Johan Tønnesen.

Pause. Sandstad enters hurriedly through the main door.

Sandstad What the hell are you playing at? (*Sees gathering.*) Pardon me, ladies. Bernick, the branch line – you have to come now or the whole scheme could collapse!

Lona Chug-a-chug, Karsten.

Pause.

Bernick I . . .

Lona Your community is waiting for you.

Pause.

Sandstad (*to Vigeland and Rummel, sotto voce*) Move.

Vigeland and Rummel rush out through the main door.

Hurry. Please. We need you.

Pause.

Johan You and I will talk in the morning, Bernick.

He exits through the garden. Bernick, half-dazed, exits through the main door with Sandstad.

Act Three

Bernick enters in a great rage through the second door, a cane in his hand. Betty follows, distraught.

Bernick He won't forget that in a hurry . . .

Betty That was cruel of you.

Bernick It's been a long time coming. I've enough on my plate without seafaring thirteen-year-olds.

Betty He's done it before.

Bernick Not in the middle of the night, he hasn't. I'm not having him stealing fishing boats – if he wants to fish, he can do it from the shore.

Betty I don't think what he does really matters to you at all –

Bernick Oh, you don't? It matters, Betty: he's my only heir. Now keep him under control.

Betty He didn't mean any harm, it's just that he's used to looking after himself –

Bernick Stop making excuses. He's confined to the house. Ssshh. (*Listens.*) Don't breathe a word.

Betty retreats. Knap enters through the main door.

Knap Do you have a moment, Mr Bernick?

Bernick (*throws away the cane*) How is it down there? Nothing wrong with the *Palm Tree*, I hope?

Knap No, she can sail tomorrow. As for the *Indian Girl* –

Bernick That bloody foreman, I warned him that if he didn't –

Knap The *Indian Girl* will sail tomorrow, too. She just won't sail very far.

Bernick What's that supposed to mean?

Knap indicates the half-open door. Bernick closes it.

We're alone, Knap. Say what you have to say.

Knap I believe Aune intends to let the *Indian Girl* sink to the bottom of the sea with all hands.

Bernick What? What are you saying?

Knap Sir, as you know, thanks to the new machines and untrained men, things have been a bit sluggish at the yard –

Bernick Yes, yes –

Knap This morning, I arrived to find they've been going great guns on the American ship. Her bottom – nothing but a gaping hole the other day – looked as good as new. Apparently, Aune's been up all night, fixing it by the glow of a lantern.

Bernick Glad to hear it.

Knap Hmm. It struck me as odd. While the men were at breakfast, I crept on board. I had a job of it, getting through the cargo, but I managed . . . and I'm sorry to report that something fishy has taken place.

Bernick I don't believe it . . . Aune's stubborn, but he's honest as the day is long . . .

Knap The truth is, the hole's been tinkered with a bit, stopped up here and there . . . but there's no new timber. Lift the sailcloth and tarpaulins and you'll find a botch-job, utter sham. The *Indian Girl* won't make it to New York. She'll plummet to the seabed like a cracked pot.

Bernick But, but – why?

Knap Our agitator has intensified his protest.

Bernick What the hell is he thinking?

Knap Wants a scandal over the new lathes and drills. New machines out, old workers back in.

Bernick And he's happy to send those men to their deaths?

Knap He doesn't think the Americans are *men*.

Bernick That's beside the point, what about the loss of capital?

Knap Our firebrand doesn't smile on capital, Mr Bernick.

Bernick Dissent is one thing . . . this is unconscionable. You'll have to take another look.

Knap Certainly, sir, but –

Bernick I need to know for certain. This is the last thing the yard needs – for God's sake keep it to yourself.

Knap If you don't mind me asking –

Bernick Find a way while they're at their lunch.

Knap – what will you do?

Bernick Report it. We can't be partners in an actual crime. I'm not having that on my conscience.

Hilmar enters through the main door.

Hilmar Morning, Karsten!

Bernick (*to Knap, sotto voce*) Confirm it first. And don't tell a soul.

Knap (*sotto voce*) Mum's the word. And you'll have confirmation.

He goes out through the garden and down the street.

Hilmar Congratulations on your triumph at the railway meeting!

Bernick Er . . . thank you . . .

Hilmar Public spirit prevails over diehard self-interest. Like the French, hailing down on the Arabs. After that embarrassing incident here, I'd have thought –

Bernick Yes, enough of that . . .

Hilmar Mind you, you haven't won the war.

Bernick Hmm?

Hilmar Down at the newspaper, Hammer's cooking up an article.

Bernick What? What do you mean?

Hilmar The new rumour. About acquisition of property along the branch line.

Bernick Who's been saying that?

Hilmar Everyone. I got wind of it at the club. Dropped in briefly, the door was open. Word is, some local lawyer has, on the sly, bought up all that fertile land on someone else's behalf . . .

Bernick Whose . . . ?

Hilmar Men at the club think it must be some confederacy from outside town; they've whiffed your scheme and nosed in there before the land went sky-high. Bloody pirates.

Bernick Don't exaggerate.

Hilmar Just calling them as I see them: pillaging outlanders. Can you believe one of our own lawyers is a sneak?

Bernick Talk, Hilmar, talk . . .

Hilmar Maybe. But talk turns into truth when it's in a newspaper, and Hammer's about to put it on the front page. The club was getting quite peevish about it. Some say they'll take their names off the lists, if it turns out to be true.

Bernick No . . . no one here would ever do that . . .

Hilmar There's only one reason these shopkeeper-types are behind you, Karsten: they want a piece of profit for themselves.

Bernick You don't know what you're talking about: there's such a thing as public spirit.

Hilmar Here? Well, you're an optimist. You judge others by yourself. But I have a sharp eye and I say, present company excepted, there isn't a man in this town who flies the flag of the Ideal. (*Heads for the veranda.*) Ugh, Americans.

Bernick Is that the captain of the *Indian Girl*?

Hilmar Looks like it.

Bernick What would they want with him?

Hilmar He's been a slave-trader and a buccaneer: peas in a pod. I'm sure they share all sorts of hobbies.

Bernick Lona and Johan don't deserve that, Hilmar.

Hilmar As I said, an optimist. If you don't mind, I'll make my escape.

He heads for the second door as Lona enters through the main door.

64

Lona Hilmar. Are you off? Is it me?

Hilmar Not at all. In a rush. A blood cousin to see. (*Calls.*) Betty!

He exits. A moment's silence.

Bernick Lona.

Lona Hello.

Bernick What do you think of me today?

Lona The same as yesterday. False colours are false colours, it doesn't matter how many you're sailing under.

Bernick My life will unravel if the truth comes out.

Lona Yes, I suppose it will.

Bernick That gossip, that crime . . . you know I'm not guilty.

Lona Of course. Who was the thief?

Bernick There was no thief. There was no robbery.

Pause.

Not a penny went missing from my mother's company.

Lona So . . . they all think Johan is the perpetrator of a crime . . . that didn't even happen?

Pause.

Bernick I'm partly to blame.

Pause.

Lona You?

Bernick nods.

Johan pretended he was Mrs Dorf's lover for you . . .

Bernick You have to remember how things stood. Don't judge me. Mother . . . she'd made such a mess of everything, so many rotten investments . . . We were plagued with bad luck, *this* close to collapse . . . I was at my wits' end . . . it was half the reason I got tangled up with that woman.

Lona Of course it was.

Bernick After you left, they concocted so many stories about Johan. That it wasn't his first affair, that he'd tried to silence Dorf with cash, that kind of thing. All this was flying about just as the house of Bernick was nearing extinction. The most natural thing in the world happened. They made a connection between the Bernick debts and Johan's disappearance to the New World. Mrs Dorf was here in the gutter, so *obviously* Johan fled to America with bulging pockets! And every time they said it, they bulged a little more.

Lona Karsten –?

Bernick I . . . I was desperate . . . I grabbed hold of that rumour . . .

Lona And spread it –?

Bernick Didn't deny it. Our creditors were hammering at the doors, I had to stop the suspicion we were in serious trouble . . . It was just bad luck, all we needed was time and our debts would be paid . . . which they *were*, in full: Lona, that rumour saved our house and made me the man I am today.

Lona A lie made you the man you are.

Bernick It didn't hurt anyone, did it? No one was meant to see Johan again!

Lona What about you? Hasn't it hurt you? Look inside yourself, tell me it hasn't.

Bernick Look inside any man you like, every one of them is hiding at least one dirty secret.

Lona Pillars of the community!

Bernick Who else is there?

Lona Who else? Who cares? What value is there in a place propped up by lies and fraud? Look at you. So respected, so powerful, lapping about in your tepid pool. You branded an innocent man – *my half-brother* – a criminal.

Bernick For God's sake, Lona . . . it nearly kills me . . . I'm ready to make it up to him.

Lona By speaking out?

Bernick You can't insist on that, you *can't*.

Lona How else can you right the wrong?

Bernick I'm rich, Lona.

Lona Buy him off? He'd spit in your face.

Bernick What's he going to do?

Lona I don't know. He hasn't said a word since yesterday. All of a sudden, Karsten, Johan has become a man.

Johan enters through the main door.

Bernick Johan –

Johan No. Me first. Yesterday, I promised I'd hold my tongue.

Bernick Yes –

Johan But yesterday I didn't know –

Bernick Let me explain, Johan –

Johan It's not necessary. I understand completely. Bernick and Company was about to fold, the infamous 'Johan Tønnesen' was all yours. I don't really have it in for you . . . we were young and stupid. But those days are over. Now I need you to tell everyone the truth.

Bernick I can't. I'm a moral man: that reputation has to stand, now more than ever.

Johan I don't give a damn about the cash-box lies, but you have to clear up the Mrs Dorf story. Because I'm going to marry Dina. Here.

Lona Really?

Bernick Here?

Johan I won't run twice. *I* want her: *you* have to clear my name.

Bernick If I confess to that, I might as well confess to the robbery!

Johan What robbery? Did you steal from yourself? The Bernick company ledgers will prove it never happened.

Bernick (*shakes his head*) The books were in a shambles . . . Even if I could prove it, what good would it do? I'd still be known as the man who saved his skin with a lie; the man who let that lie stand for fifteen years. You've forgotten who they are if you think they wouldn't hang me for that.

Johan All I know is that I have to make Mrs Dorf's daughter Mrs Johan Tønnesen.

Bernick (*wipes sweat from his forehead*) Johan, listen . . . Lona . . . we're so close to something great. Destroy me, you destroy the town's future . . . this is your home . . . something is there for the taking . . . don't compromise it, for God's sake, please don't . . .

Johan It's your future or mine, Karsten.

Lona Karsten?

Bernick It's the railway . . . it's not simple. You know about the old proposal for a line up the coast? That had a lot of support around here, especially in the newspapers. I stopped it because it wouldn't have helped our steamboat trade.

Lona The steamboat trade up the coast, you mean? In which you have an interest?

Bernick Yes, but I was above suspicion. My name, Lona, my good name.

Lona But it would have eaten into your profits?

Bernick *I'm* rich enough, I could have borne it, the real loss would have been the *town's*. So they decided on an inland line. As the ink was drying on that . . . secretly . . . I made sure a branch line could be built.

Lona Secretly? Why?

Bernick You've heard, have you, about the mineral-rich forest land . . . ?

Johan Yes, some partnership from outside town has bought it all.

Bernick For a song. The owners were scattered everywhere, the land was virtually worthless to them when they sold. If news of the line had been public, they could have named their price.

Pause.

This could be misconstrued. Only a man with a rock-solid reputation could admit to it in a place like this.

Pause.

Lona You.

Bernick nods.

Johan You bought the land? On your own?

Bernick If the branch line goes ahead, I'm a millionaire. If it doesn't, I'm through.

Lona Risky, Karsten.

Bernick I've gambled every penny on it.

Lona I wasn't thinking about your pennies.

Bernick Don't you see, Lona, that's exactly it: I'm respected, I have the muscle to do this, see it through, say to them, 'Citizens, I took this risk for you.'

Lona For them?

Bernick They won't question it.

Lona And what about the honest men who've seen no need to whisper and connive and plot?

Bernick Who?

Lona Rummel, Sandstad and Vigeland, of course!

Bernick They're in on it.

Lona Ah. Silly me. How much?

Bernick A fifth of the profits.

Lona What *pillars*.

Bernick Yes, of a community that *forces* us into this kind of racket! I had to act in secret or else everyone would have wanted a hand in it; that land would have been subdivided and mismanaged . . . these people would have botched the whole scheme. I'm the only man in this town who has what it takes to handle something so ambitious. No one has the capacity for big business here; every entrepreneur in the country is a foreigner. My conscience is clear; I've done the right thing. *I* can make that land work for the ordinary men of this town, *I* know how to make it endure; I'm the only one.

Lona You're probably right about that.

Johan But I don't know the people in this town . . .

Bernick You were born here –

Johan What about my happiness?

Bernick What about theirs?! If our story gets out, Johan, my enemies will unite, and fall on me, and tear me to shreds. Youth is no excuse: these people hold on to everything. They'll find a thousand episodes from across the years to dissect in the light of Mrs Dorf. Their slander will be the death of me; I'll be forced off the railway, *it* will go down, *I* will go down, and all of us, Betty and Olaf included, will be driven out.

> *Pause.*

Lona Johan . . . you have to leave.

Johan Fine. I'll do it. But not for ever. I'm coming back.

Bernick Stay there, Johan, I'll pay –

Johan Keep your filthy money, give me my name!

Bernick And give up my own?

Johan *That* problem is between you and your town. I have to marry Dina. I'll leave on the *Indian Girl* tomorrow.

Bernick The *Indian Girl*?

Johan Conveniently for you, the captain promised me a berth if I needed it. I'll sail to America, sell the ranch, see to my life and then come back – and the guilty man can have his guilt.

Bernick But I'm not guilty of the robbery!

Johan You've been sitting pretty on that shabby lie for fifteen years!

Bernick You're pushing me too far . . . I'm warning you . . . Go ahead, say what you like, I'll deny it. It's a conspiracy, revenge, you're here to blackmail me . . .

Lona Shame on you, Karsten.

Bernick None of it's true. I'll deny everything.

Johan You seem to have forgotten I still have the letters you wrote to me about the Dorfs. They're explicit enough.

Bernick You wouldn't . . .

Johan If I have to read them in the town square, good citizen, I will.

Pause.

I'll be in New York in three weeks. I'll stay a fortnight . . . which gives you two months to find a way out. Two whole months, Karsten. Goodbye. Love to Betty, though she hasn't been much of a sister. (*Calls.*) Marta . . .!

He leaves through the second door.

Bernick Lona . . . you have to stop him from –

Lona I think it's perfectly obvious I no longer have an ounce of control over him.

She exits after Johan. Bernick paces apprehensively.

Bernick The *Indian Girl* . . .

Aune enters through the main door.

Aune Excuse me, sir . . . are you busy?

Bernick (*snaps*) What do you want?

72

Aune I have a question.

Bernick Well, then?

Aune If the *Indian Girl* wasn't ready to sail tomorrow . . . would I definitely, *definitely* be sacked?

Bernick But she *is* ready. Isn't she?

Aune Yes. Supposing she weren't, would I be sacked?

Bernick What is the point of this, you imbecile?

Aune I'd like the answer to the question, sir.

Bernick When I say something, do I usually mean it?

Aune Then tomorrow, I'd have lost my position in my home; lost my voice on *my* side of the town, where the workmen live, where people are poor –

Bernick We've had this out already, Aune.

Aune The *Indian Girl* will sail.

Pause.

Bernick Look . . . I haven't got eyes in the back of my head . . . I can't be responsible for everything. You can assure me that ship has been repaired satisfactorily?

Aune You didn't give me much time, Mr Bernick.

Bernick I repeat: is she caulked? Is she seaworthy?

Pause.

Aune The weather's fair. It's summertime.

Pause.

Bernick Is there anything else you have to say to me?

Aune Nothing springs to mind, sir.

Bernick Then the *Indian Girl* will sail.

Aune Tomorrow?

Bernick Tomorrow.

Aune bows and exits. Bernick stands for a moment, then strides for the door as if to call Aune back. He stops, hand on the doorknob. The door is opened from the other side, and Knap enters.

Knap (*sotto voce*) Slink in to confess, did he?

Bernick Did you get on board?

Knap Does it matter? You saw the evil in that operator's eyes.

Bernick Shut up, Knap, that's impossible. Well?

Knap I was too late, they were already hauling her out of dock. All too quick for my liking . . .

Bernick What about the inspection?

Knap She passed.

Bernick Ah. You see! There's nothing to worry about.

Knap Mr Bernick, as you know, all that's a formality. They don't expect anything but a clean bill of health from *your* ships.

Bernick Irrelevant: *we* are in the clear.

Knap But Aune was obviously –

Bernick Aune reassured me.

Knap I'm convinced to the marrow of my bone –

Bernick What's this about, Knap? You don't like the man? Stick the knife in over some other issue. The *Indian Girl* has to sail tomorrow . . . she has owners, you know, it's not my decision.

74

Knap Very good, sir. But if anyone ever sees that ship again, I'll eat my hat.

Vigeland enters through the main door.

Vigeland Morning, Bernick.

Bernick Morning . . .

Vigeland Just wanted to know if you think the *Palm Tree* should sail tomorrow, as I do?

Bernick Yes, Vigeland, that's settled, isn't it?

Vigeland I've just heard from the captain they've hoisted storm-signals.

Knap The barometer's been falling all morning.

Bernick Is it very bad?

Vigeland A breeze . . . vigorous, certainly . . . but she'll be sailing *with* the wind.

Bernick What do you think?

Vigeland As I said to the captain, the *Palm Tree* is in God's hands. It's only the North Sea they've got to cross in the first place. Freight rates in England are pretty high at present.

Bernick Yes, it wouldn't be in our interest to wait.

Vigeland She's a sturdy ship. Fully insured. Not as risky as, say . . . the *Indian Girl*.

Bernick What's that supposed to mean?

Vigeland She's sailing tomorrow, I've heard?

Bernick Yes, on instruction from New York, and –

Vigeland Well, if that old carcass . . . with *that* crew . . . It'd be a bit humiliating, wouldn't it, if we decided *our* ship –

Bernick Quite, Vigeland. Have you got her papers?

Vigeland Ready and waiting . . .

Pause.

Bernick (*indicates his study*) Mr Knap?

Knap (*to Vigeland*) We'll sign off on it at once, sir.

Vigeland Good, good. And the outcome we leave to God.

He exits with Knap to Bernick's study. Rørlund comes in via the garden.

Rørlund Mr Bernick? Not out working somewhere in the town today?

Bernick (*vague*) No . . . obviously . . .

Rørlund I've come to see your wife. I thought she'd benefit from a kind word.

Bernick Yes . . . I suppose she would.

Rørlund Is everything all right? You seem out of sorts.

Bernick What do you expect? . . . Mr Rørlund, wait. I have a question.

Rørlund And I, I hope, an answer.

Bernick Suppose . . . suppose a man is about to embark on something that will benefit thousands . . . but . . . it became necessary . . . to sacrifice one?

Rørlund I don't follow.

Bernick A man of business is about to build an enormous factory. He's experienced, so he knows that one day, one of his workmen will die.

Rørlund Only too probable, I'm afraid . . .

Bernick Or . . . he opens a mine. He employs fathers, men in their prime –

Rørlund Some of whom, sadly but inevitably, will never come home to their children.

Bernick So . . . if he *knows* a thing is going to cost a human life . . . but that it's for the public good . . . one life lost in the interests of hundreds of others . . .

Rørlund You're nervous about your railway. The excavations, the detonations . . .

Bernick Yes, yes: the railway . . . and the factories and mines and water-wheels along the line –

Rørlund Mr Bernick, you're almost *too* conscientious. Put it in God's hands, then you're above reproach. Proceed: be optimistic: build your railway.

Bernick But . . . let me be specific. Suppose we have to detonate explosives in a dangerous place, or we can't build it. The engineer knows a workman is going to die . . . but it's his duty to send him to light the fuse.

Rørlund Well . . . the engineer –

Bernick Should what? Do it himself? It doesn't happen. He has to send the man to his death.

Rørlund No engineer here would do that.

Bernick They wouldn't think twice in America.

Rørlund I'm sure you're right. Corrupt and evil as *she* is.

Bernick There's a lot to be said for the place.

Rørlund Mr Bernick!

Bernick They have space, freedom, backbone; they've grasped that big things come at a price. Meantime we're locked in here, gagging on our own pettiness.

Rørlund Human life is petty?

Bernick If one gets in the way of the welfare of thousands of others.

Rørlund But this is incredible. What's got into you today? America? Lives there are as numbers in ledgers. Can you conceive of one of our shipowners sending a man to his death for the sake of profit? These big nations *knowingly* launch rotten ships –

Bernick I'm not talking about rotten ships!

Rørlund But I am, Mr Bernick. Floating coffins.

Bernick They've nothing to do it! If a Norwegian general saw a few bloody soldiers on the field, he'd wake in a sweat every night for a year!

Johan enters from the second door, followed by Dina, then Marta.

Dina Johan –

Johan It's simple –

Rørlund You?

Johan I won't give you up.

Rørlund You dare to show your face here?

Johan When I come back, you'll understand – and so will you, Marta.

Rørlund What are you saying?

Johan Slander me again if you like. She's going to be my wife.

Pause.

Marta Dina, come back to your room.

Rørlund Don't move, Miss Marta. And to let her anywhere near her. (*Calls at the second door.*) Mrs Bernick!

Lona enters.

Lona Hello, reverend.

Rørlund Miss Hessel? You haven't left town either? (*Calls.*) Mrs Bernick!

Bernick What are you doing?

Betty enters through second door.

Betty Mr Rørlund – he won't listen to me. No one will listen to anything I have to say.

Rørlund Dina. You're a rash girl. Not immoral . . . but thoughtless. I don't blame you, I blame myself.

Dina Mr Rørlund, don't. Not now.

Rørlund Yes, now. I can't hesitate any longer.

Hilmar enters through the second door.

Hilmar Oh. Still here.

Rørlund (*turns to Johan*) She is my fiancée.

Betty What?

Bernick Mr Rørlund?

Rørlund We're engaged.

Marta (*to Dina*) Please tell me that isn't true.

Lona The man's a liar.

Johan Dina?

Pause.

Dina?

Pause. Dina nods.

Rørlund First the mother, then the daughter? Get out of our town. (*to Dina*) The time had come. I believe it won't be misconstrued, I really do. (*to Betty*) We should take her somewhere quiet. We need to calm her nerves, bring her peace.

Betty Yes. Dina, my darling . . . come with me . . .

She takes Dina out through the second door. Rørlund follows.

Marta Goodbye, Johan.

She exits.

Bernick Johan . . . you . . . won't be sailing on the *Indian Girl*?

Johan I will.

Lona Don't worry, John.

Bernick But you're not coming back?

Johan I am. Now more than ever.

Lona I'll stay. And I'll keep an eye on the reverend.

Bernick After that? Why?

Johan To revenge myself on all of you. I'm going to take hold of each and every one of you and I'm going to smash you. Smash you.

He exits through the main door. Vigeland and Knap enter from Bernick's study.

Vigeland All signed, Mr – oh, Miss Hessel.

Lona I'm not here.

She exits through the main door.

Vigeland All signed.

Bernick Good . . . good . . .

Knap (*sotto voce*) And the *Indian Girl*? Any . . . change of plan?

Bernick She sails tomorrow.

He exits to his study. Vigeland and Knap exit through the main door. Hilmar is about to follow, when Olaf cautiously pops his head around the second door.

Olaf Psssst. Uncle Hilmar!

Hilmar Hello, urchin. What are you doing down here, haven't you been incarcerated?

Olaf Ssshhh! Have you heard?

Hilmar That you got a good whipping today? Yes. Thrilled me no end.

Olaf (*with a dark glance towards his father's study*) He's never going to do that to me again. I'm not talking about that. I'm talking about Uncle Johan. He's sailing with the Americans tomorrow!

Hilmar What of it?

Olaf I *should* go on a buffalo hunt, Uncle. Maybe I will.

Hilmar Don't make me laugh.

Olaf You wait, Hilmar.

Hilmar Go back to your cot, you pusillanimous little mouse.

He exits via the garden. Olaf runs out as Knap enters via the main door. He approaches Bernick's study and opens the door slightly.

Knap Mr Bernick, sorry to bother you again, but the storm-signals were justified. She's brewing.

Pause.

Is the *Indian Girl* to sail, even so?

Bernick (*from his room*) Yes. She sails.

Knap shuts the study door and exits through the main door.

Act Four

The table has been removed. Dusk. Stormy weather.
A servant is lighting the chandelier. Two maids bring in
lamps, candles and vases of flowers, which they place on
tables and stands along the walls. Rummel is instructing
them. He is wearing evening dress.

Rummel . . . every *second* candle. It's a surprise. No, no,
too many flowers, too ostentatious, he'll see straight
through that . . .

Bernick enters from his study.

Bernick What's going on?

Rummel Ah. There you are. (*to servants*) Thank you.

The servants exit through the second door.

Prepare for the proudest moment of your life. A public
parade. In your honour.

Bernick What are you talking about?

Rummel A parade. With banners. And a band. We'd
planned torches, but decided not to risk it – the weather,
you know. Though there will be illuminations . . . a story
for the newspapers.

Bernick Cancel everything.

Rummel Too late. They'll be here shortly.

Bernick Why didn't you tell me, Rummel?

Rummel Your wife's in on it. I'm setting things up in
here; she's seeing to the refreshments . . .

Bernick Is that singing?

Rummel Only the Americans. They're hauling the *Indian Girl* to the buoy.

Bernick Not this evening . . . I can't do it . . . I'm not well . . .

Rummel I can see that. You have to pull yourself together, damn it. A brilliant show of public support for you, just the thing to trounce our opposition. Sandstad and Vigeland agree. The rumour mill is at it; you can't hold off any longer, you *have* to make an announcement about the land. So, we'll have some bubbly-water and speeches, and amidst the chin-chins you can tell them all about the enormous risk you've taken in their name. These people love a gala. You can do a hell of lot during a song. But we have to set the mood, or the thing won't go.

Bernick Yes, yes –

Rummel Especially such a sensitive thing. With your name, thank God, we're home and dry. So. Hilmar Tønnesen has composed a song – something about the claims of Idealism, it's very charming – and then Mr Rørlund will make a speech. Then you reply.

Bernick No, Rummel . . . you do it . . .

Rummel Even if I wanted to, I couldn't. The speech will be to *you*. He might reserve a word for me and the others, I couldn't say. Then you propose a toast: 'To the prosperity of the community.' Then Sandstad will talk briefly about harmony between employer and worker; Vigeland will assure everyone that bursts of *steam* won't change our moral climate; and I'll tip my hat to the ladies, whose public work, though modest, is not without – for Christ's sake, man, are you even listening?

Bernick What's the sea like? Is she very rough?

Rummel The *Palm Tree* is insured, Bernick. More to the point, she's in excellent repair.

Bernick Cargo lost . . . trunks, papers . . . it doesn't always mean . . . why the singing?

Vigeland enters through the main door.

Vigeland The *Palm Tree*: out she goes.

Bernick Vigeland . . .

Vigeland Evening, Bernick.

Bernick You're a seaman . . . what do you think . . . ?

Vigeland God's hands is what I think. I've just been on board to give the crew some religious pamphlets. Can't hurt.

Sandstad and Knap come in through the main door.

Sandstad I'd bet my life on it, they're as good as dead. (*Sees gathering.*) Ah. Evening all.

Bernick Knap . . . ?

Knap Sir?

Bernick Something to say?

Knap Me?

Sandstad It's the crew of the *Indian Girl*. Four sheets to the wind, every last one. They'll never see New York . . .

Lona enters through the main door.

. . . unless New York's in Hell.

Bernick Is Johan on board?

Lona Will be soon. We just went our separate ways.

Bernick He won't change his mind?

Lona No. Firm as a rock.

Rummel (*fumbles with the curtains*) Damn these new-fangled contraptions . . .

Lona You want them closed?

Rummel I do, Miss Hessel.

Lona (*helps him*) I have to say I'd rather open the curtains on my brother-in-law . . .

Rummel You *will*, as soon as the garden is surging with people. Then they can look in on the scene: the happy first family. Pretend to be surprised, Bernick. All citizens should live in glass houses.

> *Bernick opens his mouth as if to say something but turns and rushes into his study.*

Might be an idea to go through it all. You too, Mr Knap, you're good with detail.

> *Rummel, Vigeland, Sandstad and Knap exit to Bernick's study. Lona has drawn the curtains over the windows. She is about to do the same over the glass door, when Olaf jumps down from the room above and lands on the veranda. He has a plaid and a bundle.*

Lona Sweet Je—! Olaf, you frightened the life out of me!

Olaf (*hides the bundle*) Sshh!

Lona Are you trying to break your neck?

Olaf Bye, Aunt!

Lona Olaf!

Olaf I'm just . . . I'm going to the harbour to say goodbye to Uncle Johan!

> *He runs out through the garden.*

Lona Olaf –!

Marta and Dina come in through the second door.
They're both wearing cloaks. Dina is holding a small
travelling bag.

Marta, did you just see –? Where are you off to? They'll
be here soon!

Dina I have to be with Johan, Miss Hessel.

Lona What? Dina, you're too late . . .

Johan, dressed for travelling, with a bag over his
shoulder, enters cautiously through the main door.

Johan Dina –?

Lona Johan, the ship!

Johan I had to say goodbye.

Marta (*to Dina*) Go on.

Dina I want to come with you tonight. Will you take
me?

Johan But –

Dina Please. Let me come.

Johan But I thought –

Dina Mr Rørlund wrote: he's going to announce the
engagement this evening to the whole town. I can't go
through with it!

Johan You don't love him?

Dina Of course I don't love him! I'd rather drown myself
in the fjord than marry that condescending peacock. I'm
fed up of being belittled, I'm sick to death of being
reminded that I'm pathetic and unloved and in need of
'elevation'. This is the moment: I have to leave. Please . . .

Johan Yes . . . *yes.*

Dina I won't be in your hair long. Just help me to get there . . . help me to see how they do things.

Lona (*points to Bernick's door*) Ssshhh . . . quiet, quiet.

Johan I'll look after you.

Dina No thank you, I can do that. Oh, these *women*, you've no idea, I've had letters all morning: 'What a windfall, Dina, lucky Dina; chivalrous Mr Rørlund.' They'll watch me over the rims of their moral books till I'm dead. I can't tolerate any more well-brought-up people!

Johan But, Dina . . . are you coming with me, or running from them?

Dina They say it's my duty to hate you. But I don't understand what they mean by 'duty'. I never will.

Lona And you don't have to . . .

Marta No, you don't. Go with him. Marry him.

Lona Marta?

Marta Oh, I have to speak up for once. All this convention and tradition – there's only so much we should have to stomach. Marry him. Thumb your nose at them, Dina. Do it: defy them.

Johan Well?

Pause.

Dina I'm your wife from this second, if you like.

Johan My wife – ?

Dina Wait. It doesn't mean I'm a thing you're just packing up and taking away. I have to work. I have to make something of myself, like you did.

Lona Good for you.

Johan But we're married?

Dina In my eyes, yes. In yours?

Johan Yes! Say it again.

Dina I'm your wife.

Lona You'll miss the ship!

Johan Lona . . . I need a word . . . (*Pulls her aside, talks to her urgently.*)

Marta (*kisses Dina*) I'll never see you again.

Dina Of course you will, Aunt.

Marta Listen. (*Clasps her hands.*) I want you to promise me you'll never come back to this place. Go. Know that all I've ever really wanted is to go myself. It must be beautiful, across the sea. The skies are wider and the clouds fly higher . . . I think a freer breeze will blow through your hair . . .

Dina You'll come one day, Aunt Marta.

Marta No. I have my job here. And I can see a way to live my life now.

Dina I can't imagine being without you.

Marta Oh, there are lots of things we think we need, when really we don't. (*Kisses her.*) But you'll have everything. Make him happy, promise me.

Dina (*shakes her head*) What will be, will be.

Marta Yes. Stay as you are. True to yourself.

Dina Yes, Aunt.

Lona (*puts into her pocket two envelopes Johan has given her*) Fine, John, fine . . . now get on board . . .

Johan Goodbye, Lona. Thank you. Goodbye, Marta.

Marta Goodbye, Johan.

Johan You've been a real friend.

Marta Be happy, your whole lives. Goodbye, Dina. Go, go.

She and Lona hurry them to the door. Johan and Dina run down the veranda steps and disappear through the garden. Lona closes the door and draws the curtains over it.

Lona Marta.

Pause.

You're sorry to see him go as well, aren't you?

Pause.

Marta Every summer I prayed he'd sail in. I waited and waited . . . This summer he finally did, and he didn't look twice.

Lona I take it he gave you a reason to hope, once?

Marta Yes.

Pause.

I loved him.

Lona That was quite a thing you did for them.

Marta Who better? As soon as I saw him, I knew he'd forgotten. We're meant to be the same age; it was sobering to realise that actually I'm ten years older than he is now. He's been breathing in clean air, standing in sparkling sunshine . . . he's strong and young and vigorous . . . I'm none of those things any more.

Pause.

Lona I've lost him myself. No use for the old half-sister now.

Marta He'll want you to go back.

Lona (*shakes her head*) He's desperate to be on his own. It's why I pretended homesickness in the first place. Men do away with anything that stands in the way of their happiness.

Marta Yes. They do miss the point.

Lona Which is?

Marta Not so much to be happy, as to deserve to be.

Lona Marta.

Bernick enters from his study.

Bernick Yes, makes no difference . . . I'll be ready . . . (*Shuts door.*) Ah, you. Look, Marta . . . what you're wearing, it's a bit . . . Go and change – and tell Betty to do the same. And tell Olaf to come down, he should be next to me.

Lona And smile, Marta. It's a party. It's a surprise.

Bernick Nothing too fancy, you hear? Smart . . . but homely. Quickly.

Marta Yes, Karsten.

She exits through the second door.

Lona So. The township comes.

Bernick Yes.

Lona Quite a moment. Must make a man proud.

Bernick Hmm.

Lona Newspapermen out in force.

Bernick Apparently, Lona.

Lona The whole street's to be illuminated.

Bernick You think I'm happy about it?

Lona I suppose not.

Bernick You despise me.

Lona Not yet, Karsten.

Bernick You've no right. You know nothing. This stunted backwater – you think I haven't had to give up my dreams?

Lona But you've had a hand in everything.

Bernick Scraps – it's all this lot can handle. Petty victories, trivial improvements, that's the sum of it. If I ever did anything too 'modern' or tried anything too big, I'd lose all my power. The community's pillars? Ha! We're the community's *tools*.

Lona You've learned that lesson late.

Bernick Lona . . . Lona . . . why didn't I know who you really were back then?

Lona And if you had?

Bernick I'd have never let you go and I wouldn't be stuck in this mess.

Lona Karsten: Betty.

Bernick Forget her.

Lona You chose her.

Bernick She hasn't got what I need.

Lona How would you know? You've never shared anything with her, you've never had a free and truthful relationship with her. You *allowed* that woman to buckle under the shame you heaped on the people she loves.

Bernick Lies, lies . . .

Lona Do something!

Bernick Not one in a million has the courage to be like you.

Lona To be themselves, you mean?

Bernick It's too late.

Lona But none of it's made you happy!

Bernick No. And it will bury me one day, and everyone like me. But a new generation is coming . . . I have a son . . . it's Olaf, I've been working for Olaf . . .

Lona *This* is what you call a good inheritance?

Bernick (*with suppressed anguish*) Oh, God, it's ten thousand times worse than you could imagine . . . but bad can turn to good . . . (*violently*) Who do you think you are, how could you do this to me? I'm still Bernick. You think you can get rid of me? *You will not eradicate me.*

Hilmar enters through the main door quickly and agitatedly, an open letter in his hand.

Hilmar Betty? Betty!

Bernick No . . . please . . . they can't be here yet . . .

Hilmar I've got to speak to her.

He hurries out through the second door.

Lona All this dread of 'being got rid of'? Let me tell you something. This boy . . . Johan the prodigal, whom your oh-so-respectable camp-followers shrink from as if he had the pox . . . he's made of stern stuff. He doesn't need any of you. He's gone.

Bernick And back in two months!

Lona No. He's taken Dina.

Bernick Dina . . .?!

Lona As his wife. No priest, no ceremony. Their slap-in-the-face to you and all the other model citizens around here. Oooh, I know how good it feels.

Bernick On the *Indian Girl* . . .

Lona No, the *Palm Tree*.

Bernick What?

Lona He loves her. He wasn't going to trust her to those animals.

Bernick (*runs to study*) Knap! Stop the *Indian Girl*! She mustn't sail!

Knap (*off*) She's already started out to sea, Mr Bernick.

Bernick (*laughs feebly, closes door*) For nothing . . .

Lona What do you –?

Bernick Leave me alone! Get out!

   Pause.

Lona (*produces the envelopes*) Your old letters to Johan. He gave them to me. The good name you borrowed from him, then stole, is mine.

Bernick The crowd's on its way, Lona Hessel. Do your worst.

Lona (*slowly tears the letters into pieces*) You don't know me at all, do you? I'm not here to betray you. I came to kick your conscience to life. I've failed. Speak to your town, stand knee-deep in your mucky lie, say what you like. Pick it up, Karsten. Get on your knees, scrape it up, it's the last of the incriminating evidence. You're safe. As for free or happy, God help you.

94

Bernick (*overcome*) Lona . . . why didn't you do this before? I'm through . . . my life is over.

Lona stares at him questioningly.

No. Bernick. Bernick.

Hilmar hurries back on.

Hilmar Where is she? Where is everyone? Karsten . . .

Bernick What do you *want*?

Hilmar I daren't tell you. It's Olaf. He's run away. He's on board the *Indian Girl*.

Bernick's feet give way.

Lona Oh, the silly boy, now it makes sense –

Bernick (*at the study door, frantically*) Knap –

Lona I saw him jump out of his window.

Bernick Stop her, stop the *Indian Girl* . . . whatever it takes . . . *stop her*.

Knap comes out of the study.

Knap Sir, it's impossible.

Bernick In the name of God stop that ship: *my son is on board*!

Knap Olaf?

Rummel, Sandstad and Vigeland make their way out of the study.

Rummel What – run away?

Vigeland How did he manage that?

Sandstad Nothing to worry about, he'll be sent back with the pilot.

Hilmar Not if he gets his way –

Bernick My boy . . .

Hilmar Little rat sent me this letter. He's going to hide in the cargo till they're on the open sea.

Bernick I'll never see him again . . .

Lona Karsten?

Bernick Lona . . .

Music is heard.

What's that . . . ?

Rummel The parade!

Bernick Stop it . . .

Rummel Don't be ridiculous.

Bernick I can't see those people . . .

Sandstad Bernick, remember what you have at stake.

Bernick None of it matters now . . .

Rummel On the contrary.

Vigeland The community, Bernick.

Sandstad Remember what the *four* of us have at stake.

Bernick I've lost him . . .

Lona (*to Rummel*) Will he be safe?

Rummel As houses! She's a sturdy ship, newly repaired.

Vigeland In your *own* yard.

Marta enters through the second door.

Marta They're nearly here, but I can't find Betty anywhere!

Rummel Up with the curtains, quickly. (*Motions to Knap and Sandstad.*)

Lona Karsten . . .

Rummel (*sotto voce*) That's really put the cat amongst the pigeons, hasn't it, mother and son making off at the eleventh hour? Quite contrary to the programme.

The curtains are opened. The whole street outside is illuminated. An enormous transparency with the words 'Long Live Karsten Bernick, Pillar of Our Community' can be seen. Bernick recoils.

Bernick Get rid of it . . . take it down . . .

Rummel Are you out of your mind?

Bernick They're laughing . . . mocking . . .

Sandstad Bernick –

Rummel I've had just about enough of this –

Bernick You don't understand . . . candles . . . they're not for me . . .

Lona Who are they for?

Knap (*sotto voce*) The dead?

Rummel It's not as tragic as all that, is it?

Sandstad The lad sails the Atlantic, sees New York, comes home. Worse things have happened.

Vigeland Trust in God, Bernick.

Rummel She's not going to sink. We're not Americans, are we? *We* don't send out floating coffins.

Marta What's the matter with him, Lona?

Lona I don't know. (*Looks to Knap.*)

Knap They're coming into the garden, Mr Bernick.

Rummel As if it were the marketplace!

Sandstad Well, I'll be . . . Rummel. You pulled it off.

Bernick Stop . . .

Rummel The whole town. Makes a man proud.

Vigeland Humility, gentlemen.

Lona Karsten –

Rummel There's the committee . . . Mr Rørlund! Mr Rørlund . . .

Bernick Please . . .

Lona Whatever's happened, you're going to have to pull yourself together.

The music reaches a climax. The veranda door is opened. Rørlund enters, ahead of the committee, escorted by two servants, who carry a covered basket. Townspeople of all ranks push their way into the room. A huge crowd, with banners and flags, can be seen in the garden and street.

Rørlund Mr Bernick, esteemed fellow-citizen, we're here to honour you.

Cheers from the crowd.

This is not the occasion to speak of your incomparable family, or your flawless character. This is a public tribute to your public life. Well-equipped ships sail from your yard and fly our flag in far-off seas. A band of happy workmen looks to you as father. The industrialist in you brings riches to hundreds. And now, thanks to your vision and untiring self-sacrifice, we stand on the threshold of a new age. You are the overseer of a scheme which, the practical men of the town assure us, will

98

stimulate prosperity and riches for the entire community. You are about to procure for us – I'll call the thing by its plain prosaic name – a railway.

Cheers.

We know it hasn't been easy.

Concurrence.

We know individuals – outsiders – have stolen assets that by rights belong to the conscientious citizens of the town.

Jeers.

But this shameful fact hasn't stopped you, because you know the true patriot looks beyond the borders of his parish.

Uncertain agreement.

Let your railway bring lasting good to all of us. It might cart in noxious, corruptive influences, but it can cart them out. Because we're not entirely free from turpitude . . . even today an evildoer has been expelled . . .

Some disorder, calls for silence.

. . . I mention it only to stress that in this house morality is valued even above family.

Cheers.

Bernick Please . . . enough . . .

Rørlund (*motions to servants*) The tokens.

The servants bring forward the basket. Committee members take out and present the gifts.

First man. In recognition of your altruistic achievements, a silver coffee service, to be used when we are lucky enough to be gathered under your hospitable roof. And for your seconds. Mr Rummel, a silver goblet, for raising

99

and draining during one of your rousing tributes to
seaport life. Mr Sandstad, philanthropist: an album
containing photographs of all your compatriots, from
humble worker to the Bernicks themselves. And Mr
Vigeland, godly man. For you, a book of sermons, with
de-luxe binding. (*Turns to crowd.*) Long live Mr Bernick
and his partners in the fight!

Cheers.

Lona Congratulations to you, Karsten.

An expectant silence.

Bernick Citizens . . .

Pause.

Rummel (*sotto voce*) Bernick? Now you respond.

Pause.

Bernick The truth is . . . I have to tell you . . .

Pause.

Lona Then tell them.

Bernick My God . . .

*Betty enters through the garden. She has a shawl over
her head.*

Betty Karsten.

Bernick I have to tell you . . .

Betty Karsten. I'm here.

Bernick Betty?

Rummel Your speech, speak!

Bernick I'm sorry . . . we didn't look after him . . . we let
him go . . . didn't watch over him . . .

Betty Listen to me –

Bernick He's lost . . .

Betty I've got him.

Bernick What?

Vigeland Ah!

Sandstad There, you see!

Rummel Fuss over nothing. (*to crowd*) Ladies and gentlemen, a moment please! I'll address you all shortly.

Lona He's safe?

Betty Safe.

Marta What a relief.

Knap (*sotto voce*) A godsend.

Bernick Where is he . . . where?

Betty I'm not going to tell you. Not till you've forgiven him.

Bernick But . . . how . . . ?

Betty You accuse me of not having a mother's eyes. But I do: I knew he was up to something. He let a few things slip . . . and when I found his bedroom empty I put it all together. I ran for Aune . . . we went out in his boat . . . She was about to sail, thank heaven we got there in time. We searched: he was in the hold. You mustn't punish him, Karsten.

Bernick Betty . . .

Betty Nor Aune.

Bernick Has the *Indian Girl* sailed?

Betty No, that's just it, Aune was as upset as I was . . . we were searching for so long it got dark. The pilot started complaining and Aune took it upon himself in your name to stop the ship from sailing till tomorrow.

Knap Did he?

Betty Karsten . . .

Bernick Thank God.

Rummel You're over-protective of the boy, Bernick.

Hilmar A month on the wild sea is exactly what that scrawny milksop needs, but oh, no . . .

Olaf appears at the main door.

Vigeland They're waiting.

Sandstad Someone has to speak or we'll have a riot on our hands.

Olaf Papa?

Bernick Olaf! My boy . . .

Olaf I won't do it again, I promise . . .

Bernick And I promise I'll never give you a reason. I'm the happiest man alive.

Rummel Well, excellent: the smiling family, as required.

Lona He's yours again, Karsten. But there's still the town, isn't there?

Rummel I think under the circumstances, *I* should address them.

Bernick No. I can speak for myself.

Rummel You know exactly what to say, of course?

Bernick Yes, Rummel. (*to Lona*) Exactly. (*Addresses the crowd, slow and serious.*) I beg your pardon. Fellow citizens, your spokesman just said we are on the threshold of a new age. I pray he was right. But first we have to admit something; something which, until tonight, we have exiled from this place. Truth.

Astonishment.

Mr Rørlund, thank you. Generous as your words were, they were tailored for the occasion – and these people need to know, I don't deserve them. The truth is, until this evening, I've not acted selflessly. I've always craved power, influence and status. It's been the motive behind most of my actions. My whole life, I've wanted to be king crab.

Rummel (*sotto voce*) What is he doing –?

Bernick I don't rebuke myself for it, in that I still think I can be counted as one of the town's most competent citizens.

Support.

But I do rebuke myself for resorting to foul play, simply because . . . because I was terrified of your tendency to suspect ulterior motives behind everything a man of reputation does.

Pause.

Contrary to reports, no outsiders have purchased land along the proposed branch line. I bought that land.

Murmurs of consternation.

As I speak, it belongs to me. Naturally, I've confided in my colleagues Messrs Rummel, Vigeland and Sandstad, and we've agreed –

Rummel That's a filthy lie, prove it!

Sandstad What are you insinuating? *Nothing* –

Vigeland Nothing's been agreed –

Bernick – we've agreed to form a public company to exploit the land; any one of you here who wishes to buy shares can do so.

Cheers.

Rummel (*sotto voce*) You snake in the grass.

Vigeland Damn you to hell. God forgive me for that.

Cheers.

Bernick Quiet! I've no right to your cheers. The truth is, my decision is new. I planned to keep that land for myself. It's time for you to know me. Let's all of us look into ourselves; let's begin our new age from this moment. The old one – with its jaundiced eye, double standards, sham respectability – is now a museum, open for instruction only. To it we present – what do you think, gentlemen? – a coffee service, a goblet, an album of photographs and a de-luxe book of sermons.

Rummel (*sotto voce*) Oh, yes, take my silver goblet, do . . .

Vigeland You've stolen everything else . . .

Bernick Ladies and gentlemen –

Sandstad (*sotto voce*) A Norseman's word, solid as the rocks.

Bernick – there's more.

Pause.

Earlier, you heard talk of an 'evildoer' who left our shores this evening.

Pause.

You don't know everything.

Pause.

Lona (*sotto voce*) The man ran off with his wife.

Betty What?

Bernick (*to crowd*) That man did not leave alone.

Lona (*sotto voce*) He left with his *wife*.

Pause.

(*loud*) Johan Tønnesen ran off with Dina Dorf!

Commotion.

Rørlund No, no, no, that's, that's, that's impossible . . .

Bernick She left as his wife, no priest, no ceremony. But I respect their marriage more than many others here, and I say, hats off to that man, my brother-in-law. He took the blame for something he didn't do. I have been ravaged by a lie. Fifteen years ago – you all know the story – *I* was the guilty man.

Betty (*trembles*) Karsten?

Marta (*likewise*) Johan . . .

Shock. The news is whispered from mouth to mouth.

Bernick That's the truth: the guilt is mine. I don't have the power to refute the abominable lies that followed. I can't complain. For years I rode on the back of them. If I'm flung to the dirt with them now . . . well, that's up to you . . .

Rørlund Mr Bernick, of all men. (*to Betty*) I pity you.

Hilmar Speechless.

Bernick The spectacle is over.

Rørlund It certainly is.

Bernick As for the land, I believe this: the public company should come under the overall control of one man. That way things can be worked properly. If the town generally desires it, I would be happy to be that man and I'd oversee the exploitation of the branch-line properties, and make certain they turned a profit. You know that I'm capable; that I know how to make things work. But it's your decision.

Pause.

I still have many things to atone for . . .

Pause.

. . . but they're between me and my conscience. Don't judge me tonight. We'll see on another day whether fifteen years of exertion is enough to correct one youthful indiscretion. Go home, look deep inside yourselves . . .

Pause.

. . . and he who is without sin among you, let him be the first to throw a stone. Good night!

Rørlund (*sotto voce, to Betty*) She was spoiled goods, after all. Not worthy of me. (*to committee*) Gentlemen. Let's pack up.

Hilmar And ship out.

The crowd disperses. Rummel, Sandstad and Vigeland exit, arguing heatedly amongst themselves.

Sandstad (*sotto voce*) Manager . . . I suppose that was his plan all along? He's richer than ever – and us?

Rummel (*sotto voce*) Dupes.

Hilmar slinks off through the main door. Silence. Bernick, Betty, Marta, Olaf, Knap and Lona remain.

Bernick Betty . . .

Betty I'm here.

Bernick Can you forgive me?

Betty Do you know, Karsten, for the first time since we met, I can see more than a foot in front of me.

Karsten What do you mean?

Betty For years, I thought you were mine but that I'd lost you. Now I realise you were never mine, nor I yours. I hardly recognise the thing I'm feeling – but it's hope. I think you and I might find each other, one day.

Bernick embraces her.

Olaf They're putting all the lights out!

Marta So they are, Olaf.

Betty There's no place for them here this evening.

They look to the illuminations, which are put out one by one during the following.

Bernick (*sotto voce, to Lona*) Thank you.

Lona What for, exactly?

Bernick I'm still standing because of you.

Lona Oh, I see.

Bernick What I mean is – you saw the good in me.

Lona That's true, I did.

Bernick And you saved me.

Lona You don't want me to light your name up again?

Bernick Not for the world.

Lona What happened, Karsten?

Bernick It would chill your blood.

Lona Try me, brother-in-law.

Pause.

Do you think I ever wanted anything *other* than to save you?

Bernick I don't know. If it wasn't hatred or revenge . . . The truth is, I don't understand you, and I still don't know why you came back.

Lona When you were a young man, you were decent. Good, kind. Free. Johan told me about the lie, and I knew you were a friend in need. And friendship . . . love . . . doesn't rust, does it? It's constant.

Bernick I don't deserve yours.

Lona Please, Karsten, I beg you, tell me you do. Reassure me, for heaven's sake.

Aune enters through the main door.

Aune Mr Bernick . . .

Bernick Aune . . .

Aune I just came to give you my keys to the yard –

Bernick No, no. I apologise.

Aune But the ship hasn't sailed.

Bernick And won't sail tomorrow. I didn't give you enough time. The work must be seen to properly.

Pause.

Aune Thank you.

Bernick Enough. Good night.

Aune nods and exits.

Lona Karsten?

Bernick Olaf!

Olaf Pa . . .

Bernick Time for bed. Come to me, Betty, come close. A good night's sleep, son, so you can grow tall and strong and build your own big life. And Marta, my darling sister, there you are.

Marta Will the *Palm Tree* be safe?

Bernick You mustn't worry. Our friends will make it to their new world. And we have a long day of work ahead in ours.

Lona You especially.

Pause.

Bernick Bed, family.

Betty (*sotto voce*) You will stay with us, Lona?

Olaf Good night, Aunt Lona!

Lona Good night, Olaf.

Olaf runs out through the second door.

Marta Good night, Lona.

Betty and Marta exit through the second door. Bernick follows.

Lona Karsten?

Bernick Hmm?

Lona You said there was still something between you and your conscience. You are truly young again?

Pause.

Bernick Good night, Mr Knap.

Knap Good night, Mr Bernick. Miss Hessel. Sleep sound.

He exits through the main door.

Bernick A new leaf, Lona, a new day. Thanks to you. You women are the real pillars of the community. If I've learnt anything over the past few days, it's that.

Lona Then real wisdom has eluded you, Karsten. Women have nothing to do with it. The spirit of freedom, and the spirit of truth – they are the pillars of the community.

End.

A Note on the Version

I incorporated thirty-three lines from early Ibsen drafts into this version of *Pillars of the Community* (1877). Eighteen of them were in the final act, which is often considered less successful than the final acts of the great plays from *A Doll's House* (1879) onwards. The argument goes that everything is a bit too convenient for Karsten Bernick, that his change of heart, and Lona Hessel's earnest acceptance of it, are not quite persuasive. After in-depth discussions with Marianne Elliott, for whose National Theatre production I tailored this text – and at the risk of a Lona-like box around the ears by the great man in the afterlife – I made additional minor alterations to two scenes in Act Four. These were: a delayed entrance for Betty and a brought-forward entrance for Olaf in the public speeches scene; and a delayed exit for Knap and new exits for the Bernicks in the final scene.

I made my first draft from a translation by R. Farquharson Sharp (1913), after which I worked from a National Theatre-commissioned literal prepared by Charlotte Barslund. I took encouragement from Inga-Stina Ewbank and John Barton's text for Barton's 1977 Royal Shakespeare Company production, the prompt copy of which was provided by the Shakespeare Centre Library, as it seemed to endorse many of the decisions I had made about the thirty-three draft lines. William Archer's meticulous 1890 translation was helpful on several points. I first read the play in the 1963 translation by Michael Meyer; everyone who works on Ibsen in the English language is indebted to him.